M000303135

IMAGES
*of America*

# WASHINGTON
# NATIONAL GUARD

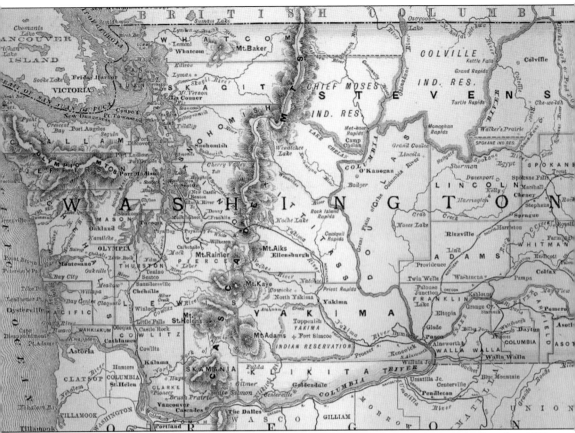

Washington looked like this on the eve of admission to the Union. Even before statehood in 1889, the Washington National Guard had begun its growth into today's 21st-century force serving the state and nation. But never did it forget its historic commitment: "Always ready, always there." (Courtesy Washington State Archive.)

ON THE COVER: Tracing its lineage back to territorial days, Eastern Washington's 161st Infantry Regiment was mobilized for service in the Pacific theater in World War II. Of those called up in 1940, these few proud soldiers, the "Dirty Dozen," stayed with the regiment all the way through occupation duty in Japan. (Courtesy Washington National Guard State Historical Society.)

IMAGES
*of America*

# WASHINGTON
# NATIONAL GUARD

William Andrew Leneweaver, Richard G. Patterson,
and Dr. William H. Woodward Jr.
Foreword by Maj. Gen. Bret D. Daugherty

ARCADIA
PUBLISHING

Copyright © 2019 by Washington National Guard State Historical Society
ISBN 978-1-4671-2985-5

Published by Arcadia Publishing
Charleston, South Carolina

Printed in the United States of America

Library of Congress Control Number: 2019941202

For all general information, please contact Arcadia Publishing:
Telephone 843-853-2070
Fax 843-853-0044
E-mail sales@arcadiapublishing.com
For customer service and orders:
Toll-Free 1-888-313-2665

Visit us on the Internet at www.arcadiapublishing.com

*This book is dedicated to all members of the Washington Army and Air National Guard, past and present, as well as to their devoted families, for their loyalty, commitment, and service to Washington State and to the United States of America.*

# CONTENTS

# FOREWORD

With great pleasure, I commend this image-rich history of the Washington National Guard to Washington's citizens, as well as to the past and present Guard family. The heritage of the Guard is wonderfully told here in a concise and personal way. The character, courage, and depth of our organization leap off the pages with vivid detail. The greater story, of course, still unfolds every day in the actions of Washington Air and Army National Guard members serving their local communities and the nation's purposes around the world.

—Maj. Gen. Bret D. Daugherty, Adjutant General
Camp Murray, Washington

# ACKNOWLEDGMENTS

The authors would like to thank the entire staff of the Washington National Guard State Historical Society; the National Guard Association of Washington; the Washington State Historical Society; the University of Washington Library, Special Collections staff; the Tacoma Public Library, Northwest Room; the Kittitas County Historical Museum; the 41st Infantry Division Association; and the 25th Infantry Division Association.

Special thanks go to Maj. Keith Kosik, Judy Dries, Birgit Leneweaver, Anne Patterson, and Tina Woodward.

The authors would also like to recognize Anne Drain Frazor and the families of Gustav Schlimmer, Perry Franklin, John Dawson, Samuel Chernis, Harry A. Comeau, as well as the Maj. Gen. Lilburn Stevens family and members of the Maj. Gen. George Haskett family. These, and many others, too numerous to mention here, contributed significantly.

Unless otherwise noted, all images used in this book are from the archives of the Washington National Guard State Historical Society.

# INTRODUCTION

Why do we do it?

Why would Andy Leneweaver leave his young family to serve with a Joint Special Operations Task Force in Djibouti in 2003?

Why would Rick Patterson leave a convenient day job to join a Public Affairs Detachment in Kosovo in 2000?

Why would Bill Woodward scramble to cover his history-professor duties when alerted that he would take his History Detachment to the Persian Gulf in 1991 (though the final call never came)?

Why would so many of our comrades—past and present—enlist, train, deploy, serve in harm's way and, yes, die to defend their state and country?

Why do we serve in the Guard? We continue a proud tradition.

The thousands of men and women of today's Washington Army and Air National Guard serve their state and nation as an operational force and dedicated civic organization. But their heritage traces back to the creation of Washington Territory in the 1850s, and to a common need and a common idea.

That common thread runs from ancient communities through the organized militias of colonial times to the modern National Guard. Homes and families face external threats; to protect their own, people must band together in legitimate armed formations. Put simply, a society's safety is anchored in its citizen-soldiers. In the words of the Constitution's Preamble, citizens should be willing to take up arms to "provide for the common defense."

History records various forms of militias: in ancient Egypt, Greece, and Rome, in medieval times, and into early modern kingdoms. However, the true ancestor of today's National Guard was born on December 13, 1636, when the Massachusetts Bay colony decreed that all able-bodied males between the ages of 16 and 60 must join the militia. Other English colonies followed suit: survival depended on constituted authorities compelling every man to serve in the common defense.

When American colonials determined that to protect their just rights, they must fight for independence, they at first relied on militia forces. Fearful of "standing armies" and reluctant to yield power to a central government, they only grudgingly created a Continental Army. A year before declaring independence, and a month after appointing Virginia militia colonel George Washington as commanding general, Congress resolved that "all able-bodied effective men, between sixteen and fifty years of age in each colony, immediately form themselves into regular companies of Militia, to consist of one Captain, two Lieutenants, one ensign, four sergeants, four corporals, one clerk, one drummer, one fifer, and about 68 privates."

The militia ideal faced real difficulties: officers had to provide their own weapons, ammunition, horses, and equipment; enlistments were short; each state retained control of what was essentially a local defense force. Even so, the militias gave crucial support to the Continentals from Boston to Yorktown.

With independence won, the Founders, still wary of a professional military and committed to the militia as the bedrock of freedom, turned to the task of creating a national government. The United States Constitution of 1787 empowered Congress

> To provide for calling forth the Militia to execute the Laws of the Union, suppress Insurrections and repel Invasions; [and] To provide for organizing, arming, and disciplining the Militia and for governing such Part of them as may be employed in the Service of the United States, reserving to the States respectively, the Appointment of the Officers, and the Authority of training the Militia according to the discipline prescribed by Congress. (Article I, Section 8 (15–16))

Accordingly, Congress periodically passed Militia Acts mandating state organizations, authorizing the president as commander in chief to call them to federal service, and providing funds for arms and equipment.

Through the early 1800s, state militia formations served with mixed performance in conflicts with Indian tribes and in the War of 1812. In the 1840s, the first wave of Oregon Trail pioneers trekked to the Willamette Valley. The 1846 Oregon Treaty set the 49th parallel boundary. Settlers soon trickled north of the Columbia River, and in 1853 a separate Washington Territory was established.

It was in this context that Washington's first volunteer territorial militia was created. The first territorial governor, West Point graduate and Mexican War veteran Isaac Stevens, called on the Territorial Legislature to enact a Militia Act. America "depends on the patriotism and the valor of its citizens for defense," he argued. "An efficient militia system is especially necessary in this Territory, which, on the occurrence of war, must, for a time, almost entirely rely upon itself."

Not until January 1855 did the Territorial Legislature pass a bill. Several militia companies were finally formed when Stevens's pressure on native tribes to sign over their land provoked a hostile response. Sporadic outbreaks brought the volunteers into the field alongside Regular Army units for some months.

Six years later came another call for volunteers—from Pres. Abraham Lincoln. The First Washington Volunteer Infantry spent the Civil War years manning posts in the Territory to discourage Confederate sympathizers and curb tribal unrest.

The decades after the Civil War saw explosive growth in the West. Railroads brought a surge of economic development. Population grew. Washington finally gained statehood in 1889. And a permanent National Guard emerged, impelled by both domestic unrest and international crises.

The process began with wealthy private citizens organizing and paying for volunteer militia companies to deal with labor and racial unrest. Adj. Gen. Rossell G. O'Brien, regarded as the father of the National Guard of Washington, arranged the first summer encampment in 1885, persuading several companies to participate at their own expense. In 1888, the Territorial Legislature provided the first public funds. Over the next several years, Guard companies were called to protect against looting after a wave of urban fires and to augment the police in labor disturbances.

By the end of the century, the nation, too, needed the Guard. At the outbreak of war with Spain in 1898, Pres. William McKinley assigned volunteer quotas to each state. The Washington National Guard signed up en masse; a regiment of infantry served for nearly a year in Spain's Philippine colony. Before they arrived, the Spanish defenders had been routed, leaving the Guardsmen to help suppress a nationalist guerrilla uprising.

Not only did the experience introduce the Washington soldiers to a wider world, but it also exposed serious flaws in the nation's defenses. The first decade of the new century thus became years of modernization for both the regular forces and the National Guard. The newly assertive foreign policy of Pres. Theodore Roosevelt dispatched the American battle fleet around the world and built modernized coastal defense fortifications. Reform of the Army included legislation to integrate state militia forces into the national defense establishment.

That mandate for a key role for the National Guard in the nation's defense was finally formalized in federal law in 1903. The legislation retained the nominal "unorganized" militia—all able-bodied males in each state—but transformed all organized state militia units into a federal reserve: henceforth the National Guard would be a trained force that could be mobilized for federal service. From this act came the Guard's unique "dual mission," a state force available to the governor until called into federal status by the president.

In practical terms, Guard units received increased federal funding and equipment and, in return, came under federal standards for training and organization. The act required 24 drill periods plus a five-day summer encampment each year, the latter with pay for the first time. In addition, Guard units would now conduct maneuvers with the active Army.

Taking the logic one step further, the Army created a Coast Artillery Reserve Corps (CARC) to augment federal coastal defense garrisons (including newly built forts at the mouth of the Columbia and the entry to Puget Sound). The first Washington Guard CARC company was activated in Tacoma in 1909. The state also constructed permanent armories and established a regular training ground south of Tacoma, which would soon become its headquarters, Camp Murray.

As storm clouds of war loomed over Europe, these systematic upgrades came to fruition in America's backyard. As a complication of the Mexican Revolution, an insurgent named Pancho Villa raided north of the border in 1916. Pres. Woodrow Wilson ordered the Army to the Southwest and mobilized National Guard elements. The Army's pursuit of Villa proved fruitless; meanwhile, more than a thousand Washington Guardsmen spent three months conducting routine patrols out of their camp at the border town of Calexico, California.

Their homecoming was short-lived. Within a year, they again mustered in their armories. This time their destination was Europe. In July 1917, the War Department picked Guard units from several states to compose a new 41st Infantry Division, dubbed the "Sunset Division." Mobilization came in August, and advance elements of the division began arriving in France by December. The 41st functioned mostly as a combat replacement and training division, though its artillery fought at the front.

Demobilization in 1919 brought the return of Washington's Guardsmen to a state confronting a sharp economic downturn and explosive tensions among union workers. Bitter labor strikes erupted again during the Great Depression of the 1930s, requiring Guard call-ups for state service. On the positive side, a new aerial photo-reconnaissance organization aided local communities.

With the onset of World War II in Europe in 1939, the United States cautiously stepped up military preparedness. On September 16, 1940, the same day the Selective Service Act went into effect, Guard units across the country were called to active duty "for one year of training." The 41st Division, made up of Guard units from Northwest states, spent a miserable soggy winter in a tent city at "Swamp Murray." A year later, the troops learned of the Japanese attack at Pearl Harbor. They were in for the duration.

The Sunset Division fought hard and well in some of the fiercest combat in the Southwest Pacific theater. So did the 161st Infantry Regiment, fighting as part of the 25th Division after reassignment. Coast Artillery regiments manned coastal defense installations and a new tank battalion fought in Europe.

Victory brought the boys home again, and again it took some years to reorganize. The 41st Division returned to its several Northwest states. The Washington Air National Guard was born as part of a separate US Air Force. These developments were shaped by the larger context of an emerging Cold War, which wrought a massive reorganization of the whole US national security apparatus.

Airpower not only required a separate service, but it also made coast artillery obsolete. Instead, Anti-Aircraft Artillery (AAA) units were created, just in time for the Korean Conflict in 1950. The 770th and 420th AAA Gun Battalions, along with the 66th Field Artillery Group and the entire Washington Air Guard, were mobilized. In 1951, the 116th Fighter Interceptor Squadron became the first jet squadron to make a transatlantic crossing, flying from Spokane to England. After Korea, AAA units became part of a nationwide air defense program employing full-time Guard battalions to augment the active army. The program soon transitioned from guns to missiles.

The turbulent 1960s brought crises at home and abroad. The 1041st Transportation Company was federalized during the Berlin Wall Crisis of 1961. From 1965 to 1969 (during the peak years of the Vietnam War), 14 units were designated as a Selected Reserve Force, drilling twice as often, in anticipation of a call-up that never came. From time to time, units were called to civil disturbance duty.

Reorganizations continued. In 1968, the 41st Division was broken up into individual brigades; Washington's major command thus became the 81st Separate Infantry Brigade. In 1974, the last missile unit deactivated, an infantry battalion became an armored battalion, and a direct affiliation with the 9th Infantry Division at Fort Lewis began.

Underlying all this reshuffling was the enhanced importance of reserve forces in the post-Vietnam era. For reasons both strategic and political, the Johnson administration had chosen to fight the Vietnam War with draftees, keeping the Guard at home. That approach changed in the Nixon years, with the end of the draft, to a concept known as "Total Force": henceforth the nation would need its National Guard to go to war. In the 1970s and 1980s the concept moved from slogan to reality: Guard soldiers would no longer stay at home while draftees went into battle; instead, with conscription ended, they would have to be ready to fight in a few short weeks after mobilization.

Thus, for the Persian Gulf War in 1990/1991, several Washington Air and Army Guard units were federalized. Later in the decade, some units deployed as part of the NATO federal peacekeeping missions in the former Yugoslavia. Then in the aftermath of the terrorist attacks of September 11, 2001, Washington Guard personnel immediately stood up for airport and border security and air refueling. Others were among the first forces sent to Afghanistan. Repeated overseas deployments followed, beginning in 2004 with the largest call-up of Guard forces since World War II. Since then, tens of thousands of Washington Army and Air Guard men and women have deployed to more than a dozen countries around the world supporting the Global War on Terror.

During more than a half-century under "Total Force," the Washington National Guard, despite repeated deployments and the high demands of its enhanced federal mission, has never forgotten it is still the state militia. Over the last several decades, the Guard has served faithfully during episodes of disaster and disorder. Most dramatic was the unique recovery effort following the May 1980 eruption of Mount St. Helens. One of the largest state call ups for wildland firefighting in Washington Guard history occurred in 1994. Guard troops mobilized in late 1999 to assist law enforcement during the "Battle of Seattle" street protest against the World Trade Organization. Guard soldiers and airmen also helped in humanitarian relief efforts in Louisiana, Mississippi, and Alabama. Most recently, the Guard aided local authorities in search and rescue after a massive landslide near Oso in 2014.

From the Palouse to the Puget Sound, from the Lingayen Gulf to the Persian Gulf, the "dual mission"—state protective force and operational federal reserve—of Washington's Army and Air National Guard lives on. Its members continue to serve state and nation, true exemplars of "Citizens Serving Citizens with Pride and Tradition."

# One

# SETTLERS TO STATEHOOD
## 1850s TO 1889

From its official birth in 1853, settlers in Washington Territory faced conflicts with local tribes. Each incident would spark interest in organizing militia companies. But lack of up-to-date weapons, equipment, organization, and leadership hampered the effectiveness of an ad hoc volunteer militia.

The 1854–1855 territorial legislative assembly passed the first law providing for a territorial militia. Further, it appointed George Gibbs of Steilacoom as brigadier general, charging him to recruit volunteer regiments. Before Gibbs could act, armed tribal resistance erupted both east and west of the Cascade Mountains. Gov. Isaac Stevens issued a proclamation calling for volunteers to quell the uprisings. Thus began the first action of Washington Territory's earliest citizen soldiers. By the late 1850s, when Regular Army troops took over, the Treaty Wars—so called because Stevens's pressure on tribes to sign treaties, giving away their lands, provoked retaliation—gradually diminished, leaving a sad legacy of death and distrust on both sides.

When the Civil War broke out in 1861, regular soldiers were ordered back east. Gov. William Pickering tried to organize a Washington Territorial Militia in response to President Lincoln's call for volunteers. Sparse population stalled the effort. But later, a volunteer regiment that included soldiers from Oregon and California was raised on War Department orders.

Native American uprisings recurred in the 1870s, mostly in the new territories of Idaho and Montana. Although Regular Army forces again bore the brunt of the fighting, Washington Territory officials successfully requisitioned obsolete arms from the regulars to equip companies of volunteer militia that stood by throughout Western and Eastern Washington.

By the 1880s, these units reached a sufficient level of permanence to warrant camps of instruction to "further perfect and better establish the esprit de corps" of the territory's scattered forces. By 1886, interest developed to the point of organizing two full regiments of infantry, one east and one west of the Cascades.

This more enduring structure meant that soldiers would be at hand to protect the mushrooming population in two urban crises: when Chinese residents of Tacoma and Seattle were targeted by rioters in 1886 and when a series of devastating fires ignited across the territory in 1889. As statehood neared, a permanent National Guard of Washington was born.

Pres. Franklin Pierce appointed West Point graduate and Mexican War veteran Isaac I. Stevens (1818–1862) as first governor of Washington Territory. In his concurrent role as US Indian agent, Governor Stevens toured the territory, harrying tribes into signing treaties to give up their ancestral lands. After each treaty, settlers swarmed into Indian country, leading tribes to resist, often with armed raids. Stevens dealt with these "Treaty Wars" until 1857, when he won election as Washington's territorial delegate to Congress. As a brigadier general in the Union Army, he would be killed in 1862 at the Battle of Chantilly.

Congress carved Washington Territory out of Oregon Territory in 1853. As shown in this 1860 map, the new domain included present-day Washington, Idaho, and western Montana. The region was rich in natural resources; as settlers began to exploit minerals, soil, and timber, they increasingly came into conflict with local tribes. (Courtesy Washington State Archive.)

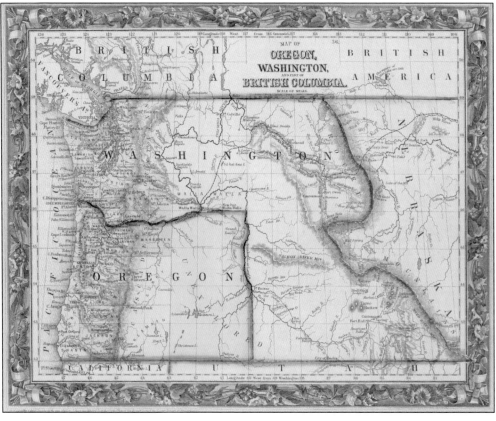

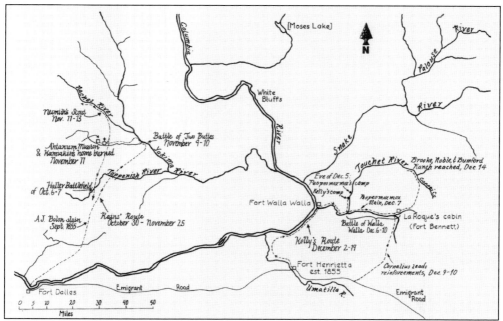

Volunteer militia companies formed to defend the settlers. This map of eastern Washington Territory highlights key sites in the 1855 campaign, the first phase of the periodic wars of the 1850s. The volunteers augmented Regular Army forays as well as marching independently and manning defensive blockhouses. Tribal resistance was finally subdued by the regular forces in 1858, but Army leaders, not unfairly, blamed the settlers for the outbreaks of violence. Another sad chapter was thereby added to the North American story of native-white armed clashes. (Courtesy Washington State University Press.)

James Tilton (1819–1878) received a presidential appointment as surveyor general of Washington Territory. Because they were old Mexican War comrades, Governor Stevens appointed Tilton as Washington's first territorial adjutant general, overseeing several of the hastily raised volunteer companies. Tilton's first (and virtually only) official act was to catch a steamer to the young village of Seattle to borrow muskets and ammunition from a US Navy warship anchored there; he quickly stepped down in 1856 as fighting petered out.

Civil War veteran Rossell G. O'Brien (1846–1914) is considered the father of the Washington National Guard. In July 1870, he accompanied the newly appointed governor, Edward S. Salomon (1836–1913), a Jewish immigrant and distinguished Civil War general, from Chicago to Olympia. Though Salomon soon left, O'Brien settled in Olympia, where he organized a militia company, "The Capitol Guards." He advanced in public service and militia rank and, in 1884, was appointed adjutant general. He led the embryonic National Guard of Washington through its early years and into the state's first half-decade. O'Brien is credited by some with originating the custom of standing for "The Star-Spangled Banner" while at a Civil War veterans' meeting in Tacoma in 1893.

Other voluntary militia companies formed themselves. By August 20, 1885, the first encampment of the Washington Territorial Militia could be conducted on Chambers Prairie near Olympia. Without provision of law for such encampment, only an "invitation to attend at their own expense" could be extended. Three units showed up: O'Brien's Capitol Guards, the Seattle Rifles, and the Queen City Guards of Seattle. Families often accompanied their militiamen to these earliest camps. (Courtesy Catalog ID 2018.0.142, Washington State Historical Society, Tacoma, WA.)

From the earliest days, militia encampments emphasized tactical military training, such as this skirmishing drill.

With Indian conflicts ending, the militia in Washington, as across the nation, began to focus on social unrest in a rapidly industrializing America. The Chinese were an early target of white working-class discontent throughout the West. In 1886, labor hostility in Seattle and Tacoma led locals to try to forcibly expel Chinese residents. Gov. Watson Squire called on the Seattle Rifles to protect the Chinese and restore order.

Fires in the 1880s prompted another service, which has endured: guarding the lives and property of fellow citizens. The first of such episodes of public protection came in 1889. Devastating fires swept through the wood-frame downtown cores of Seattle, Vancouver, and Spokane. Militia companies responded to provide security for the devastated areas. The militia's presence was not just for show. Here, soldiers in Seattle detain a suspected looter. From this public protection assignment until today, the Guard has helped to preserve public order, but always to augment, never to substitute for, law enforcement.

A soldier helps to guard rolling safes and vaults recovered from Seattle's burned-out banks and other businesses. Many banks that survive today began after the fire to provide rebuilding capital.

Seattle was not the only fire victim. Late in June 1889, a series of fires destroyed the business district of Vancouver. Then, on August 4, Spokane suffered an equally destructive fire, which once more required the militia's protective services. A soldier from the city's 2nd Regiment, commanded by Brig. Gen. A.P. Curry, stands guard. Mayor Fred Furth had instructed General Curry to "take entire charge of the city and surroundings and guard the same." The mayor pledged that "the police force would assist and act on [Curry's] suggestions." (Courtesy Northwest Museum of Art and Culture.)

## THE WESTERN UNION TELEGRAPH COMPANY.

This Company TRANSMITS and DELIVERS messages only on conditions limiting its liability, which have been assented to by the sender of the following message.
Errors can be guarded against only by repeating a message back to the sending station for comparison, and the company will not hold itself liable for errors or delays in transmission or delivery of Unrepeated Messages, beyond the amount of tolls paid thereon, nor in any case where the claim is not presented in writing within sixty days after sending the message.
This is an UNREPEATED MESSAGE, and is delivered by request of the sender, under the conditions named above.

THOS. T. ECKERT, General Manager.                                                                 NORVIN GREEN, President.

Dated Olympia. Executive Mansion Washington 11
To Gov Elisha P Ferry

The president signed the proclamation declaring Washington to be a state in the union at five oclock and twenty seven minutes this afternoon

Jas G Blaine

Better news came at the end of that deadly year: a telegram dated November 11, 1889, from Secretary of State James G. Blaine notifying the territory that Pres. Benjamin Harrison had signed the proclamation declaring Washington to be the 42nd state. Anticipating the wire, Elisha P. Ferry was immediately inaugurated as Washington's first state governor. Parading at the celebration was Tacoma's legendary Cavalry Troop B of what was now the National Guard of Washington State.

# Two

# MILITIA AT HOME TO NATIONAL GUARD ABROAD
## 1890 TO 1899

Militia companies had focused on fraternal good times and local needs. With statehood they gelled to become an official and permanent National Guard of Washington. By the end of the decade, Washington soldiers were fighting overseas on a national mission.

In 1890, the new state's militia—now rightly named "National Guard"—consisted of 17 infantry companies and two cavalry troops, with an infantry regiment and cavalry troop located on each side of the Cascade Mountains. But public funding amounted to a paltry tax levy, totaling a mere $43,400.

Hence, a local unit initially had to function as a sort of self-supporting local club or society. The captain was "chairman" as if of a civic organization. Other officers served as treasurer, secretary, and so on. An able-bodied male citizen could become a member of the society by enlisting and making "application," but approval had to be secured from the members by ballot.

In October 1890, a convention of officers, in accordance with state law, elected Rossell G. O'Brien as adjutant general, with rank of brigadier general but without salary. Throughout the decade, whether to select the adjutant general by appointment or by election created controversy.

In October 1894, the legislature increased the Washington Guard to 2,327 officers and men. Despite this expansion, and even though many towns sought to organize their own companies, the total number of authorized units stayed the same.

The increase in strength and status was tested at both ends of the decade. Labor troubles continued to require the Guard to aid local authorities, as in a mineworker strike in the King County coalfields in 1891.

Then, in April 1898, the Spanish-American War broke out over Cuba. Pres. William McKinley called for a volunteer force, assigning quotas to each state. In a matter of days, Washington's Guardsmen had oversubscribed the levy. They deployed not to the Caribbean but rather, along with Guard regiments from other Western states, to Spain's Philippine Islands colony. Ironically, by the time they reached Luzon, Spanish rule had been overturned, and the Guard volunteers were ordered to fight a frustrating counter-guerrilla war against stubborn Filipino nationalists.

Their service in the far Pacific from December 1898 to August 1899 was an apt precursor to repeated calls to duty in the dawning 20th century.

The coming of statehood accelerated the transition from an official but rather haphazard volunteer militia to a permanent National Guard. The newfound status gained visible expression in public ceremonies featuring fancy uniforms (most privately purchased). Here, Gov. Elisha P. Ferry (first row, center right) poses with his adjutant general Rossell O'Brien (seated on the governor's right) and the governor's staff officers. The full-dress uniforms differentiate infantry from cavalry (horsemen flaunting gaudy plumage on their headgear). Military tents reveal that the occasion is an annual summer encampment. (Courtesy Catalog ID 2011.0.86, Washington State Historical Society, Tacoma, WA.)

In the transition from militia to National Guard, a nationally distinguished career officer was an attractive candidate for adjutant general. A noteworthy example is Frazier A. Boutelle (1840–1924). Boutelle, today singled out for his African American ancestry, began his nearly 60 years of military service during the Civil War, retiring (for the third and final time) at the end of World War I. Among other military postings, he served as superintendent of Yellowstone National Park, where he fought to save the bison. In 1896, Washington Republican governor John McGraw appointed him the state's first nonelected adjutant general. But politics still ruled: the 1896 election of a Populist governor ended Boutelle's term.

In the later 19th century, the National Guard emerged throughout the United States as a key arm of law enforcement amidst increasing labor unrest. Washington State's resource-based economy was fertile ground for labor militancy. In the coal district of south King County in the summer of 1891, unionized miners went out on strike. The Oregon Improvement Company, a Northern Pacific Railroad subsidiary, imported black coal miners to break the work stoppage. To defuse the explosive situation, the Guard was called out. Company C, 1st Infantry Regiment, from Tacoma, poses in Gilman (now Issaquah), probably on Main Street (now Andrews Street). King County deputy sheriff John F. "Jack" McDonald, in civilian clothing, is fourth from left.

Guard troops stand by their tents, erected in classic military formation at Gilman.

An economic depression hit in 1893, and heightened labor tensions continued to affect the Washington Guard, even indirectly. The 2nd Infantry Regiment stands at "parade rest," probably next to the first National Guard armory in Seattle. They were late arriving at their annual encampment due to a Northern Pacific Railroad strike. Commanding the regiment is Lt. Col. Michael McCarthy, Medal of Honor recipient while in regular service.

Cavalry Troop B from Tacoma conducts stable duties during a summer camp on grounds that later became Camp Murray. Many of the animals were personally owned by the cavalrymen. The pony in the center may have been a troop mascot.

Late in the decade, American engagement abroad enlarged dramatically, culminating in the Spanish-American War of 1898. The Washington Guard provided a regiment to fight in the Philippines. Young US Army lieutenant John H. Wholley (1868–1912), an 1890 West Point graduate and a professor of military science at the University of Washington, was appointed commander of the 1st Washington Volunteer Infantry. Here, Colonel Wholley sits astride his horse on Murray Creek near American Lake, where the troops staged for their overseas service.

As untested as their commanding officer, Washington National Guard soldiers trained before deploying in a temporary bivouac dubbed Camp John Rogers, in honor of the governor. Colonel Wholley instituted a strenuous training program and Army discipline. When a popular company commander from Centralia was disqualified for medical reasons, some of his men refused to serve under a different officer. Colonel Wholley dismissed the entire company but invited the men to reenlist. (Courtesy University of Washington yearbook, 1900.)

Arriving in Manila in November, the regiment faced a tense standoff. The US Navy had overthrown Spanish rule, but Filipino nationalists expressed outrage that the United States decided to assume a colonial role. Above, the Washington soldiers deployed south of Manila at an old Spanish blockhouse guarding a main access route, overlooking an ironically named Concordia Creek. The road crossed a bridge that marked the boundary between US occupation and the nationalist-dominated countryside. At first, an uneasy peace prevailed as Filipino and American sentries took up posts at opposite ends of the span: American on the right, Filipino at left. The concord dissolved on March 4, 1899. An incident elsewhere on the American perimeter triggered a coordinated Filipino attack. Below, the regiment returned fire from their jerry-built defensive positions. (Courtesy University of Washington Libraries, Special Collections.)

Soon came the command to counterattack. Above, soldiers vaulted from their trenches, splashed across the creek, formed a deadly firing line, scattered the attackers, marched into the village of Santa Ana, and took the Filipino command post. Below, following the successful charge, soldiers returned to the blockhouse (at right). But a frustrating months-long campaign had only begun. Repeated forays into the interior to suppress pockets of nationalist resistance would be followed by a pullback to defensible lines. The campaigning lasted through the summer, when orders came to return home; Regular Army formations took over for what would prove to be a long and ugly Philippine-American War. (Courtesy University of Washington Libraries, Special Collections.)

The homecoming after the year in federal service was triumphant, crescendoing to a celebratory end. Exhibiting pride in their service, these Guardsmen pose for a studio photograph after their return. All are armed with their individual rifles and display campaign medals on their uniforms. The collar of the officer at center prominently displays "NGW," for "National Guard of Washington."

Here, the colors of the volunteers proudly fly at a formation of Company M troops from Centralia. Note that the regiment has sewn its moniker on the stripe just below the star-field of the national flag. Washington's citizen soldiers knew they had proven themselves a true *national* Guard. A new century would test that new role.

# Three

# NATIONAL GUARD TO DUAL-MISSION FORCE
## 1900 TO 1916

The Spanish-American and Philippine-American Wars exposed serious flaws. To defend a new global empire, the Army was reorganized, the Navy expanded, and coastal defense fortifications built.

Integral to these reforms, masterminded by Secretary of War Elihu Root, was recognition of the key role of the National Guard. The Militia Act of 1903 established the Guard not just as a state force but also as a federal reserve, with federal funding and federal oversight.

A concurrent reorganization of the Washington Guard included a system of examination of officers and frequent rigid inspections. In that same decade, the state legislature funded construction of permanent state armories from Spokane to Aberdeen, and a more systematic approach to training developed.

As early as 1901, the prairies around American Lake came under consideration to become the prime training grounds for the Army's Western Department (all Regular Army troops plus Guard units from Idaho, Oregon, and Washington). In 1904, the present-day Camp Murray site was selected. Major Army and Guard joint maneuvers took place there over the next several years.

Meanwhile, six federal forts were built to defend the entryways to the Columbia River and Puget Sound from the modern "blue water" steam and steel navies deployed by the great powers. But how to find enough soldiers to man all the new gun batteries? A 1902 report proposed that the "militia . . . supplement the regular force in manning the coast defenses in time of war." Accordingly, several Washington Coast Artillery companies were activated as part of a new Coast Artillery Reserve Corps; they trained alongside the regulars at the various coastal forts.

Then, in 1910, a Washington Naval Militia was commissioned, soon reaching 286 officers and men, and given training vessels. Absorbed into the Navy during World War I, the Naval Militia of Washington disappeared, replaced by a fleet reserve program.

The Great War had erupted in Europe in 1914. Voices in neutral America began calling for enhanced military preparedness, and Congress agreed. Adj. Gen. Maurice Thompson reported that "the Federal Act . . . will necessitate quadrupling the present strength of the [Washington] National Guard" to the level of "5,600 men."

In June 1916, President Wilson mobilized the dual-mission Guard, though not yet for the conflict raging across the Atlantic. It was to deal with a closer threat: a raider from revolutionary Mexico named Pancho Villa. The 2nd Washington Infantry Regiment mustered into federal service. But instead of joining Gen. John Pershing's Punitive Expedition into Mexico, the Washington troops settled into a cycle of border guard duty and rigorous training at Calexico, California. Anticlimactically, they mustered out on October 8, 1916.

Still, the deployment did serve to introduce them to new mechanized tools of war. And they had experienced a hint of what lay ahead. On April 2, 1917, the United States ended its neutrality by declaring war against Germany. The Yanks were coming, and that would include the Washington National Guard.

In 1903, the annual National Guard summer encampment was conducted on the broad, lightly wooded plain next to American Lake, south of Tacoma, that would later become Camp Murray—first the storage arsenal and then the headquarters of the Washington National Guard. Earlier that year, the state had purchased 220 acres; in 1904, the War Department chose the site for maneuvers by both regular and militia formations.

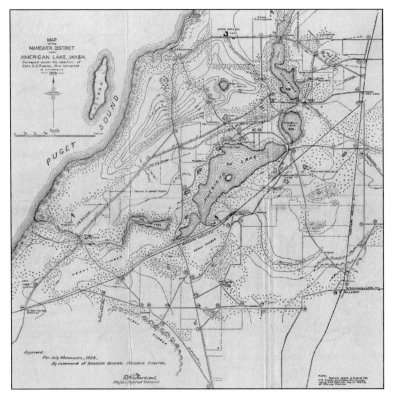

The joint maneuvers of 1904 were the largest military gathering and exercising of troops in the Pacific Northwest to date. Over 4,000 Guard infantry, cavalry, signal corps, field artillery, hospital, and other elements from Washington, Oregon, and Idaho trained alongside the Regular Army force, which included the African American "Buffalo Soldiers" of the 9th US Cavalry. This map depicts the "American Lake Maneuver District."

James A. Drain (1870–1943), shown here about 1915, was appointed by Gov. Henry McBride on January 16, 1901, as brigadier general and adjutant general of the Washington National Guard. Born in Kirkwood, Illinois, in 1870, General Drain enlisted in the Washington Guard in March 1894 and rose through the ranks, earning appointment as a major in November 1899. He was a self-taught lawyer and accountant who brought the concept of a "dual-mission" National Guard from Washington State to a joint War Department–National Guard meeting in Washington, DC, that hammered out the new Militia Act of 1903, also known as the "Dick Act" in honor of its congressional sponsor. (Courtesy Anne Drain Frazor.)

Drill and ceremony remained crucial parts of annual summer encampments. Parade skills have long been considered essential to instilling esprit de corps and discipline in soldiers, as well as to developing a leader's ability to direct troops with confidence.

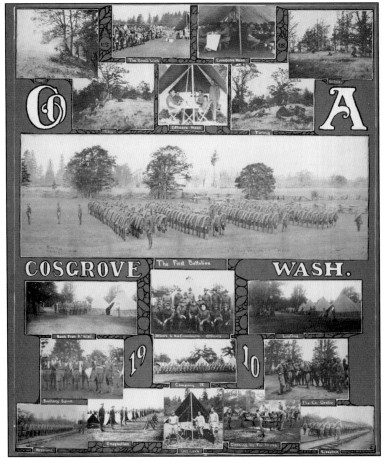

Tacoma's Company A, 1st Battalion, 2nd Washington Infantry Regiment, memorialized their 1910 training in this photograph card. The images provide a good idea of what "summer camp" was like. That year's camp was named in honor of Gov. Samuel G. Cosgrove, who had died in office the year before.

The new permanent state armories built in this era, in Washington and elsewhere across the nation, were reminiscent of medieval military structures in Europe. The first, at Second Avenue and McClellan Street in Spokane, was completed October 1, 1907, at a cost of $58,360.06. Although now an entertainment venue, this same Spokane armory is still recognizable from Interstate 90 for what it was.

The Bellingham armory, completed June 1, 1911, for $74,401.27, stood at the corner of Pine and Elk (now State) Streets. It became a storage facility owned by Western Washington University.

The crews of the newly created Coast Artillery Reserve Corps prepare a charge and ram it into the breach of this 10-inch gun at Fort Casey about 1910. Though never called upon to engage a hostile navy, these installations survived as training facilities through the mid-1940s.

This soldier takes a break while sitting on a massive 10-inch shell stockpiled in an underground ammunition magazine.

US Navy cruiser USS *Concord*, an obsolete 230-foot veteran of the Battle of Manila Bay, was assigned to the new Washington State Naval Militia in 1911. Here, in the summer of 1915, militiamen of the 1st Division "swab the decks" of the *Concord*, a routine chore while aboard their floating barracks. Other ships—USS *Wyoming*, USS *New Orleans*, and USS *Milwaukee*—served as training ships.

But most notable was the USS *Vicksburg Gunboat No. 11*. Launched on December 5, 1896, she saw combat during the Spanish-American War in Cuban waters and then sailed with the Asiatic fleet, followed by patrolling off the Central American and California coasts. She then laid up at Puget Sound Naval Shipyard for repairs in 1912, after which came duty with the Washington Naval Militia as a training vessel. That service occupied her until World War I, when she again served in combat. After use as a Coast Guard training ship, she was scrapped in 1946.

Col. George Lamping (1875–1951), shown on his beautiful mount, commanded the 1st Washington Infantry. Before commissioning as a colonel and regimental commander in 1901, Lamping served in the Philippines. He left the command in 1909 to accept appointment as adjutant general by Gov. Samuel Cosgrove, serving until succeeded on January 1, 1911, by Fred W. Llewellyn.

Maurice Thompson (1878–1954) was the longest serving adjutant general in Washington State with the fifth-longest tenure in US history. His career began with enlistment as a private in Company B, 1st Washington Volunteer Infantry, in July 1898. Commissioned an officer, he rose through the ranks until May 1, 1914, when, as a major, he became adjutant general. After overseeing the mobilization of the Washington Guard for World War I, Thompson was ordered to active duty. He was reappointed adjutant general in 1921. He retired in 1941, following mobilization of the Guard for World War II. In 1945, Thompson was again selected as adjutant general, this time to prepare for the reconstitution of the Washington Guard following the war. He retired for good in 1949 with a combined 29 years as adjutant general.

In 1908, Capt. E.H. Norton (1881–1958) stands before his command, Company D, 2nd Washington Infantry, just a short distance from where the new Seattle armory would open the following April. The pictured building at 2114 Western Avenue, perhaps the company's temporary home, became a Guard parking annex. Today, it is listed by Seattle's Department of Neighborhoods as the historic "Rainier Boarding and Livery Stable/Armory Garage."

The men of the "Fighting Co 'K' NGW" from Walla Walla posed for this photograph while "at mess." Note that several are not in uniform, which was not unusual for the time because military uniforms were in short supply. Recruits were equipped as far as possible from surplus stores on hand at each company station.

When Pancho Villa conducted raids into the United States, the 2nd Washington Infantry Regiment was mustered into federal service. The regiment, with a strength of 61 officers and 2,069 enlisted men, established camp at Calexico, California, in July 1916. Once on the Mexican border, Washington Guard infantry, signal corps, and cavalry endured the summer heat, dust, and hardships during their active federal service, which was not particularly active, confined to guard duty and border security.

They kept busy with regular calisthenics, an unavoidable part of daily drills. This kept the men fit and helped maintain discipline and readiness amid the tedium.

During this expedition, the Army pioneered the use of motorized trucks, whose mobility, endurance, and speed far exceeded the ability of the conventional horse-drawn wagon to haul ammunition and other supplies.

As a US military vehicle, the motorcycle made its first operational appearance during the Mexican border affair. Useful for delivering messages, the new contraption proved especially worthwhile in the desolate country around Calexico.

This photograph is of Capt. Harry A. Comeau (1886–1954) and his first sergeant in the captain's quarters. One imperative of life for Army leaders is paperwork, even in the field. It is a curse and a necessity. Captain Comeau and his first sergeant—typewriter at the ready—were not exempt from daily reports.

At the completion of their duty at the Mexican border in September, the troops were eager to get home. The return train trip up the West Coast must have seemed like a dream after months of dust, dirt, heat, repetitious duty, and long hours of boredom. Here, troops hang from the windows, excited to finally head home. But another call-up would soon come.

# Four

# THE GREAT WAR, TO EUROPE AND BACK
## 1917 TO 1919

The return of Washington soldiers from the Mexican border coincided with Pres. Woodrow Wilson's campaign for reelection. Wilson stressed that "he kept us out of war." He won, but he soon led the nation into the Great War in Europe, calling the Washington Guard back to federal service as part of the American Expeditionary Force (AEF) in France.

Why the reversal? Wilson sought peace based on certain international principles—freedom of the seas, for example—but Germany defiantly unleashed its submarines against American shipping. Congress declared war in April 1917. National Guard units across the country waited.

Fifteen years of Army modernization and integration of the Guard, culminating in the Mexican mobilization, assured that the AEF would deploy well prepared. Already in early 1917, states had stationed armed guards to protect armories and military stores. In Washington State, the adjutant general ordered elements of the 2nd Infantry Regiment to mobilize at their armories, while the entire Washington Guard began an intense recruiting drive.

But the call did not come. Neither equipment nor training sites for a flood of new soldiers existed. And the Army struggled through a complete revamp of its force structure. The AEF's commander, Gen. John "Black Jack" Pershing, insisted on creating huge new "divisions"—28,000 strong, twice the size of Allied divisions—comprising four massive infantry regiments.

Finally activated July 18, 1917, Guard formations from Washington and other states merged to create the 41st ("Sunset") Infantry Division. Washington contributed its infantry regiment and new field artillery battalion—now designated the 161st Infantry and 146th Field Artillery—plus cavalry, signal corps, a field hospital, and some coast artillery companies.

When the 41st Division arrived in France, it was assigned to process newly arriving soldiers for frontline units—eventually, after the Armistice of November 11, 1918, reversing the flow to get the doughboys home. Thousands of Washington's Guardsmen shipped to the front as replacements, while its signal units trained new arrivals, and cavalry performed military police duty.

However, the field artillerists remained intact. The first AEF Heavy Field Artillery regiment to disembark in France, the 146th saw its first combat in July 1918, remaining constantly in action at the front until joining the Army of Occupation in postwar Germany.

Coast artillery companies served initially at Puget Sound forts; some were dispatched to Montana to quell labor unrest. In mid-1918, they went to France but saw no action.

Following their return, many Washington Guardsmen mustered out at newly established Camp Lewis adjacent to Camp Murray (now Joint Base Lewis-McChord). The 41st Division, reconstituted, lived on as an umbrella organization for postwar Guard units in the Northwest states.

Well prior to call-up, in fact even before Congress declared war, rigorous training began at National Guard armories and field sites across the state. At Camp Murray, the 2nd Washington Infantry assembled in March for pre-mobilization field training. Additional units of cavalry, signal corps, coast artillery, and a field hospital, as well as the Washington Naval Militia, also mustered.

In April, Battery A, field artillery, assembled at Fort Walla Walla. The fort had been shuttered back in 1910, and the War Department claimed that the United States no longer owned it. Only after much dickering with government officials could Adj. Gen. Maurice Thompson convince the feds that they really did still own the old fort. Among those mustering in were three typical doughboys from Eastern Washington: Gustav Schlimmer, Battery F, chemical weapons noncommissioned officer; Samuel L. Chernis, Battery A, machine gunner; and Perry S. Franklin, Battery F, artilleryman. Their journals help personalize the story of service in the Great War.

Meanwhile, with the 2nd Washington Infantry anticipating federal service, intensive recruiting began. This temporary and impromptu station on a Spokane street corner exploited words of General Pershing himself to drive the campaign.

A key aide to Thompson in the Fort Walla Walla dust-up was Paul H. Weyrauch (1874–1937), who had served at the fort as an active second lieutenant before retiring to live in town. Soon after the April declaration of war, Weyrauch, now recalled to active service, lobbied for a full battalion of field artillery to be organized east of the Cascades. After much correspondence, he was released to accept a commission as major of field artillery in the Washington National Guard. Arriving back at Walla Walla on July 18, Major Weyrauch set about to recruit and organize the battalion.

Troops from the 2nd Infantry clean mess kits as they settle into their training regimen at Camp Murray.

World War I introduced deadly new weapons, including mustard gas and phosgene (the cause of most gas deaths). Learning to don the M2 protective mask before deploying overseas was essential training. The French-made M2 was used by French, British, and American troops throughout the war. Once at the front, Gus Schlimmer recorded how an ammo dump took an incoming shell, releasing deadly phosgene that caused several casualties. Sam Chernis was one who suffered a mustard attack.

Multiple threats to life and limb explain why the field ambulance was another key piece of modern equipment on the western front. Most were custom-built on a Ford Model T chassis with wood litter-carrying racks. They were operated by the US Army Ambulance Service, which began as a volunteer organization. (Courtesy Schlimmer family.)

Nicknamed the "Liberty Truck," the Class-B standardized military truck was built in the thousands, though only a small number made it to the front lines. These 41st Infantry Division trucks were fitted out with searchlights, canvas-covered cargo beds, and spoke wheels with solid hard-rubber tires.

Cpl. Samuel Chernis (1895–1942) of Walla Walla chronicled the artillery's story. A salesman at the Empire Furniture Company, he enlisted in Battery A on July 23, 1917. After discharge in June 1919, he returned to Walla Walla and Empire Furniture. He was instrumental in founding his hometown American Legion post, becoming its first commander. (Courtesy Chernis family.)

On October 9, Sam's battalion left Walla Walla for the east on a 15-car Pullman-equipped special train. The pleasant trip across the United States featured regular stops for exercise, including ball games between the various batteries. Three hot meals each day were served from baggage cars equipped as kitchens. On October 16, the battalion finally arrived at Camp Greene, its assembly station near Charlotte, North Carolina.

At Camp Greene, the battalion joined with other artillerists to form the 146th Artillery Regiment, part of the 66th Field Artillery Brigade. Then, it was on to New York, from which the soldiers sailed on December 24 aboard the SS *Lapland*. The vessel had been requisitioned and converted to a troopship the previous June.

On board was another 19-year-old artilleryman, Cpl. Gustav Schlimmer (1895–1968) of Odessa. Gus had enlisted in the Washington Guard a few months earlier. While in France, he compiled a war photograph album that included notes of his training, operations, movements, and personal experiences. A week out to sea, Gus penned the following: "Tues., January 1, 1918, New Year's Day aboard ship. We had a big roast goose plus drinks. Played cards all night. Had a nice day aboard ship." (Courtesy Schlimmer family.)

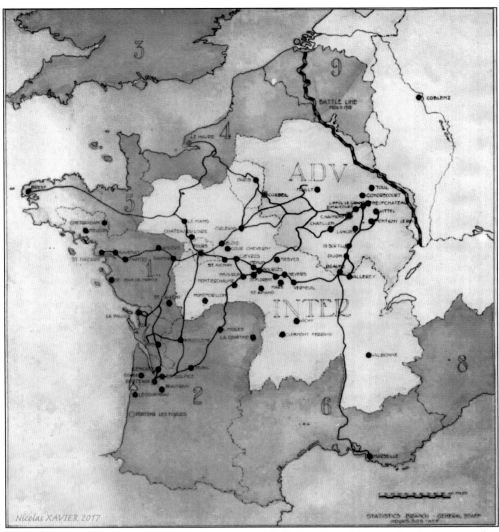

The AEF arrived with the war stalemated just inside France's northeastern border, as traced at the edge of the "advance" zone. Le Havre on the north coast and St. Nazaire on the west coast were the primary ports of entry. Because early arriving US divisions were woefully understrength, the 41st Division served as a "depot division," processing inbound materiel and men (including their own) for movement to the front. The "Sunsetters" were located strategically in the heart of France between Tours and Bourges, in the "intermediate" zone about 100 miles south-southeast of Paris. Their base was at St. Aignan, center. (Courtesy Nicolas Xavier.)

One who was dispatched to the battle area was Capt. Harry Comeau, who was assigned as an "observator" with the 206th French Infantry. A Mexican border veteran (see page 38), he deployed as commander of Company A of the 161st Infantry Regiment. Above is Captain Comeau's bilingual American Expeditionary Forces identity card. At right, he stands between French officers near Verdun. City officials honored him with its Book of Gold medal for his work with the 206th.

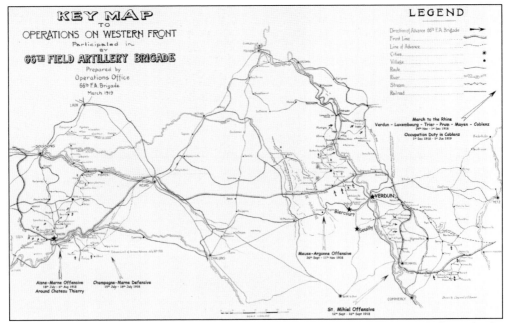

Unlike their parent division, the 66th Artillery Brigade moved intact to the battle front, fought at Chateau Thierry (left), and then moved via Reims and Verdun to St. Mihiel (right). After the armistice, the brigade proceeded from Verdun into Germany, reaching as far as the Rhine River at Coblenz.

Cpl. Gus Schlimmer and pals pose for a group photograph, possibly at Camp De Souge, where they trained on their new Canon de 155 Grande Puissance Filloux mle 1917 (GPF) guns. During off hours, Gus investigated the local area. He wrote, "Met some Frenchmen who can talk English. We have a class in one of the French cafés, and I pick up a few more words of French." (Courtesy Schlimmer family.)

The French GPF was quickly pressed into American service to remedy a shortage of big guns. Weighing 14 tons, it fired a projectile over six inches in diameter more than 12 miles. Upon arrival at the training site Camp de Souge, Gus's and Sam's 146th Field Artillery Regiment learned they had been converted into a motorized artillery regiment equipped with this gun—the first US unit to use it. (A 1918 version can still be seen outside the American Legion post in West Seattle.) Sam was not impressed and wrote the following: "Our No. 1 gun blew up on July 13, 1918, caused from poor ammunition. It was the 6th shot fired by the piece." (Courtesy Franklin family.)

Besides such occasional misfires, a major challenge was moving these massive guns. The Army's field artillery tractor was a solid but clumsy piece of equipment. This version was made by the Holt Manufacturing Company; another American model was built by the Chandler Motor Car Co. (Courtesy Franklin family.)

Hygiene was always a problem in the trenches; when opportunity arose, troops washed their clothes. The chore harkened back to days when the local nearby creek or watering hole was the only choice. Here, a 146th Field Artillery soldier, a French woman, and two French soldiers scrub in a local pool.

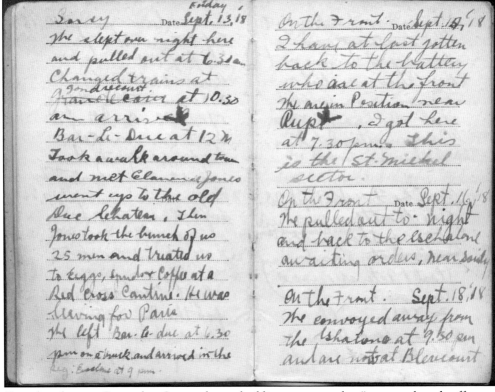

On a short leave in September, Sam and some buddies were treated to "eggs, spuds and coffee at a Red Cross Cantina" before returning to the front near Belrupt-en-Verdunois in the Saint-Mihiel sector. Not for long, however. Soon, they were on the move again—first to Souilly and then north to Nixéville-Blercourt, about 13 kilometers southwest of Verdun. (See map on page 48.)

Field communication initially could as easily be by messenger pigeon or by signal flag as "by wire." But fast-changing technology meant those older tools were yielding to telegraphs, telephones, signal lamps, and radio. Still, dogs and horses were often used to lay the cables and telephone wire.

Artillerymen of the 146th are seen with their beast of a truck, probably a 3.5-ton Kelly-Springfield. Pride shows with their "cross-cannon" insignia painted on the side. (Courtesy Franklin family.)

Pfc. Perry S. Franklin (1895–1966) of Spokane served in Battery F, 146th Field Artillery. Below, Perry (far left) and comrades pause before muscling a 155-millimeter shell into the open breach of a GPF field gun, under camouflage near Nantillois, on the Meuse-Argonne front. (Courtesy Franklin family.)

At the front, Battery F soldiers pose on their 155-millimeter gun. Though the fighting would soon end, the artillery brigade would be ordered to move into Germany on occupation duty. (Courtesy Franklin family.)

Perry made the following notation: "This is our 3rd gun, you can see the holes in the trail which were made by German shell exploding about 10 feet away from it. We lost several men by the exploding of that shell." (Courtesy Franklin family.)

Throughout the campaigns, the Yanks could never forget who they were. In 1918, the battery had marked the Fourth of July by marching on parade at Clermont-Ferrand in central France.

Inspecting 41st Division troops, General Pershing (1860–1948), AEF commanding officer, is joined by the suited Newton D. Baker Jr. (1871–1937). As President Wilson's appointed secretary of war, Baker gave oversight to the whole US Army during World War I.

War's end! Sam Chernis duly recorded that on "November 11, 1918. The last shot was fired on this date at 10am. . . . The Germans at last came to their senses" and agreed to "Peace Terms." (Courtesy Chernis family.)

On the Front Date Nov. 10, '18

The Escalone was moved today up about 3 kilometers past Banthonville.

Nov. 11. 1918. The last shot was fired on this date at 10 am.

On the Front Date Nov. 11, '18

Today at 11 am on the 11th day of the 11th month in the year of 1918. The germans at last came to their senses and excepted all Peace Terms. of the Allies and signed an armistice.

Soldiers of the 41st Division (note their "sunset" shoulder patches) receive recognition and praise from their commander, Maj. Gen. Hunter Liggett. In October 1918, Liggett took command of the 1st Army and directed the final phases of the Meuse-Argonne offensive.

The exultant sign says it all, as these soldiers from E Battery, 146th Field Artillery, leave no question where they are headed. (Courtesy Franklin family.)

As the doughboys closed out their service, they also closed out their diaries. For the 146th, that did not happen until after several months in occupied Germany. Not until June 1919 could Sam Chernis record this page in his closing chapter. He debarked at the French port of Nazaire, docked at New York City, and staged back at Camp Merritt. After enlisting in the Washington Guard's Battery D on July 23, 1917, Sam had trained at Fort Walla Walla into October, departed New York on Christmas Eve, joined the AEF in France, then fought across the now-silent battlefields of World War I. Now, finally arriving back home in Walla Walla, Sam happily signed off with a simple, "Here I Am." (Courtesy Chernis family.)

# Five

# WORLD WAR TO
# WORLD WAR
## 1920 TO 1940

After the Great War, the United States retreated to isolation, disarmament, and neutrality, largely gutting its capacity to wage war abroad.

But not the National Guard. Sustainment of the interwar Guard gave the nation a trained skeleton force when the Axis powers rose.

In the 1920s, units returned home to reestablish as National Guard organizations. With reconstitution came changes in missions and mechanization.

World War I had vaulted Washington State into the nation's political, economic, and cultural mainstream. Now, the state became a key contributor to national security strategy as well. Wartime Camp Lewis became permanent Fort Lewis. Naval facilities on Puget Sound remained active. And Boeing began manufacturing warplanes.

The Boeing story illustrates a strategic revolution. The Great War had added air combat to land and sea. The next war would find airpower decisive. Washington would be in the vanguard. This new mission came to the Washington Guard in an unusual way. Spokane ponied up $10,000 to claim a new aerial observation squadron. Under a legendary stunt pilot, Maj. Jack Fancher, the 116th Observation Squadron quickly became a dashing presence across the region as it produced aerial photographs for civilian clients.

Ground units also served the state during both disasters, like fires and floods, and civil disturbances. In 1926, a fire at the Walla Walla penitentiary required Guardsmen to prevent mass breakouts. Both in 1919 and again in the mid-1930s, hard economic times aggravated longstanding tensions between industry and labor; when dangerous unrest erupted, the Guard augmented local authorities.

The Great Depression of the 1930s provided a surprising boost: membership surged amid rampant unemployment. Pres. Franklin Roosevelt's New Deal funded new armories across the state.

The old 248th Coast Artillery Regiment drilled faithfully, though seacoast guns were clearly obsolete. But elsewhere, innovation brought not only the air squadron but also other new functions like a medical regiment with motorized ambulances, a tank company, and more. Most poignant of these changes, and most symbolic of interwar transformations, came when Tacoma's historic Troop B had to trade in its beloved horses for motor vehicles.

Old vied with new in the interwar decades; the new prevailed. The Washington Guard was ready when everything changed in September 1940.

Few World War I veterans rejoined their old Guard units. The 41st Division, now officially reallocated to its several Pacific Northwest states, had to reconstitute from new recruits. By 1920, the 146th Field Artillery resumed its annual encampments, concluding with this grand pass-in-review. But it had to train with out-of-date equipment, relying on horse-pulled cannons,

6 F. A. Camp Murray, Wash. 1921. Col. H. G. Winsor, Commanding

caissons, and limbers, long since superseded on the front in France. Eventually, as another world war loomed, tractors would replace horses, paralleling adoption of radio communication, fully armored tanks, modern medical support, and successive generations of aircraft.

By contrast, the future was already at hand by 1924 in the Spokane Valley, home of the 116th Observation Squadron, 41st Division Air Services. Its first commander, Maj. John T. "Jack" Fancher (1891–1928), above center, shakes hands with a Spokane official; the unit enjoyed strong support in the city. Fancher grew up on a Spokane farm. He pursued a business degree at the University of Washington, where he starred at basketball. When the United States entered World War I, Fancher enlisted, quickly seizing an offer to attend flight school. After serving as a combat pilot, he returned to his farm. But soon, Adj. Gen. Maurice Thompson, who had goaded city leaders into raising funds for military aviation, tapped him to lead the new squadron.

In 1927, Major Fancher flew to New York to persuade organizers to hold that year's National Air Races in Spokane. On his return flight, he visited Pres. Calvin Coolidge (left) at his summer home to lobby for aviation. Fancher's advocacy paved the way for a northern air route from Minneapolis to Spokane, eventually a main corridor for Northwest Airlines.

The squadron's mission was aerial reconnaissance, using custom high-altitude cameras. They applied their skills to serving the community. The Spokane flyboys provided aerial photographs for *National Geographic*, helped the Spokane sheriff chase criminals, conducted searches, and helped fix the site of the future Grand Coulee Dam. And in 1931, they were showcased in a spectacular airshow complete with mock dogfights and a precision flyby.

The squadron boasted this famous patch. Legend has it that Lt. Laurie Heral came up with the concept during a late-night poker game. He threw down the ace of spades, known to all as the "death card," then took out a dagger and drove it through the center of the card. The ace-and-dagger insignia has endured as the emblem of the 116th and successor organizations.

A lineup of 116th aircraft: two PT-1s and an O-17 (both built by Consolidated), and a Douglas O-2C. From 1928 to 1934, the PT-1 Trusty was the primary trainer, replacing the initial fleet of Curtis JN-6-A2 Jennies. The O-17 was a more advanced trainer used from 1928 to 1934; it featured wheel brakes and improved landing gear designed for rough field operations. The O-2C, an observation aircraft, flew from 1926 until 1931.

It was the Douglas O-38 that became the 116th's mainstay, flown in various configurations throughout the 1930s. This E model was powered by a 625-horsepower R-1690-16 radial engine driving a metal prop. Note the ace of spades prominently displayed on the engine cowling.

In 1932, the 116th Photo Section posed at Felts Field wearing obsolete uniforms in front of an obsolete airplane. By 1939 (below), pilots sported leather flight jackets emblazoned with the ace of spades in front of a sleek North American O-47 single fixed-wing observation aircraft. This airframe, powered by a 1,060-horsepower Wright R-1820 engine, had replaced the Douglas O-38.

Headquarters Troop – 24th Cavalry Division escort to the Governor.

On the ground, meanwhile, the old Army still shone at ceremonial affairs. In full regalia, Tacoma's Troop B cavalrymen, enjoying their last few years as horse soldiers, in 1932 were called on to escort Gov. Roland Hartley of Everett. By contrast, innovation and modernization accelerated elsewhere. Mounted cavalry, "leg infantry," and horse-drawn artillery were fading away, replaced by wheeled and track-driven vehicles. The M2A3 "Mae West," a twin-turret tank with two machine guns and thicker armor, anticipated the ferocious tank battles of the global war to come. (Above, courtesy Tacoma Public Library.)

Company C, 161st Infantry, falls in during its 1935 encampment. Regular inspections of soldiers in formation could be followed by meticulous scrutiny of equipment. This two-soldier pup tent with gear laid out awaits the sergeant's nitpicky eye.

In the summer of 1935, in the depths of the Great Depression, up to 30,000 timber workers across the state walked out for better pay and union recognition. But the unions themselves were locked in a heated rivalry pitting the Communist-oriented National Lumber Workers Union and the less radical American Federation of Labor–affiliated Sawmill and Timber Workers Union. Gov. Clarence Martin called out the Guard to preserve order. The strikers viewed the soldiers as lackeys of the millowners, especially when the Guard was tasked with escorting strikebreakers across the picket lines. As sporadic violence culminated on July 12 at Tacoma's Eleventh Street Bridge, Washington Guardsmen confronted the strikers with tear gas and fixed bayonets. Guard soldiers were also dispatched to Aberdeen and Hoquiam; in the latter town, a Superior Court injunction banned any Guard interference with picketers. By early August, the timber companies made grudging concessions, workers filtered back, and Guard troops demobilized. Immediate gains for labor were slight, but the long-term impact was significant, including union suspicion of the Guard.

Further evidence of the embrace of the new came in packages both small and large. The "walkie-talkie" radio went through many iterations before being fielded in units throughout the Army. Think of this model as the "cell phone" of 1935.

New community-based armories continued to rise across the state to meet the Guard's training, housing, and equipment-storage needs. The Aberdeen armory, completed in 1922, went through several updates in the 1930s. Sadly, a massive fire tore through the building in June 2018.

Illustrating 1930s upgrades to older structures, and starkly highlighting the Guard's transformation to a modern force, the old horse cavalry arena of the Tacoma armory became a truck garage—and just in time. Tensions rose rapidly after 1938 in both Europe and Asia. While Japan pummeled China, Hitler moved eastward. The Nazi blitzkrieg hit Poland in August 1939, and World War II was on. Would the United States be drawn in? Active military strength was under 335,000. When America awakened, the Guard was ready.

## Six

# WORLD WAR II, TO THE PACIFIC AND BACK
## 1940 TO 1945

Hitler invaded Poland in September 1939. Another world war had begun. The United States, officially neutral and woefully unprepared, tried to rebuild its arsenal while aiding the Allies.

A year later, the president activated the multistate 41st Division for an announced year of training. The good-hearted citizen-soldiers sang, "Good-bye dear, I'll be back in a year." But a Japanese attack would stretch that year to five.

By the time the Guardsmen from Washington, Oregon, Idaho, Wyoming, and Montana assembled at Camp Murray, recruiting had raised the division's strength to nearly 14,000. The troops spent a miserable fall and winter, suffering from influenza and global uncertainty, as the Nazis rampaged through Europe and Japan menaced the Pacific. By November 1941, Washington's 161st Infantry Regiment received orders to reinforce US troops in the Philippines. En route, soldiers learned the shocking news from Pearl Harbor. Orders changed. Bloody combat in the South Pacific lay ahead.

As Japanese forces swept southward, Australia lay defenseless, its army fighting the Axis in the Mediterranean. Army chief of staff Gen. George Marshall chose the 41st Division to step into the breach, the first American division to deploy. Before departing, the division slimmed down to just three infantry regiments. In this streamlining, the 161st Infantry Regiment was reassigned to the newly activated 25th Infantry Division.

Once Australia was secured, elements of the 41st Division went on the offensive, first along the north coast of New Guinea in January 1943. Soon dubbed "MacArthur's Jungleers," the division slogged through desperate fighting from Salumaua to Biak Island. They then jumped to the southern islands of the Philippines.

After the Japanese surrender, Gen. Douglas MacArthur assigned the 41st Division to occupy the area around devastated Hiroshima. At inactivation on December 31, their total service had stretched to the longest of any US division. Many survived, but jungle warfare took a heavy toll: nearly 5,000 casualties, including a thousand dead.

Meanwhile, the 25th Infantry Division, anchored by the 161st Regiment, had entered combat at bloody Guadalcanal. Extended heavy combat followed on Luzon in the Philippines, marked by both individual and unit heroism. The 161st Regiment, too, performed occupation duty, in southern Honshu, until November 1.

Coast artillery and flying units also mobilized, eventually deploying along the Pacific coast from Los Angeles to Alaska. An outlier was the 803rd Tank Destroyer Battalion. A latecomer to mobilization (February 1941), it consolidated several units, including old Troop B, and won honors in Europe.

41st Infantry Division soldiers began arriving at Camp Murray in September 1940, under mobilization orders issued by Gov. Clarence Martin, for a supposed one year of training. As soldiers fell into training routines and mundane duties, their "uniforms" were not uniform. The soldier at right sports a World War I helmet, web belt, pistol holster, and boot-legging; his buddy gets by in blue denims, vintage service cap, and common work shoes. Innovative quartermaster officers reportedly shopped for work denims from the local Montgomery Ward stores. Even so, soldiers had to wait until arrival overseas for a full kit.

A shared wood-floored canvas tent became a soldier's primitive new home. Canvas cots ringed a remarkably ineffective wood stove. (Some soldiers squeezed a retail potbelly into their cramped quarters.) And, in one soldier's understatement: "Not the greatest chow."

Life in a tent city was far from ideal. As chilly fall rains began, cutting firewood became a daily chore. The following winter would prove unusually wet, turning the orderly tent city into a soggy, gloomy, unhealthy "Swamp Murray."

Weapons training was paramount for all soldiers. First came knowledge and care of one's own weapon, checked at regular inspections, like this one for the 161st Infantry Regiment in early 1941. Then, training expanded with instruction on both individual and "crew-served" weapons, like the 30-caliber and 50-caliber machine guns. Such training ramped up to daily drills as deployment overseas loomed.

Next came target practice on a firing range, a central feature of all military training, especially when real combat lurks down the road ahead.

Training day began with early-morning calisthenics. Company E, 116th Medical Regiment, from Seattle, forms up in a mishmash of uniforms.

April 12, 1941, was Easter Sunday. Friends and family joined the men of the 41st Infantry Division for services at Camp Murray. Chaplain M.M. Patten, joined by Maj. Gen. George White (division commander) and Gov. Arthur C. Langlie, conducted the service at a makeshift chapel. (Courtesy Tacoma Public Library.)

The old coast artillerists discovered a new mission against a new weapon using even newer technology. The recently created 205th Coast (Antiaircraft) Artillery Regiment, called to active service in February 1941, now pointed its palisade of 90-millimeter guns at the sky, not the sea. To track and target fast-moving aircraft, they employed an automatic fire-control system integrating telescopic range-finder mechanisms and a newly invented "electric director"—a merging of first-generation radar and computer technologies. The 205th and its older cousin, the 248th, dispersed their constituent elements to guard coasts from Los Angeles to Alaska to Scotland.

Tensions were rising in Asia by the fall of 1941. The United States needed to shore up the defenses of the Philippines and ordered the 161st Infantry Regiment to entrain for San Francisco, where they would board ships for the far Pacific. The cars rumbled southward. Shortly after noon one Sunday, the train stopped for a few minutes near Klamath Falls, Oregon. The stationmaster rushed out: "Say, have you guys heard the (Japanese) have bombed Pearl Harbor?!" It was December 7, 1941. The regiment instead headed for Hawaii and assignment to the newly activated 25th Infantry Division.

Following the Pearl Harbor attack, Imperial Japanese forces swiftly conquered the Philippines, threatening Australia. The 41st Infantry Division, under Brig. Gen. Horace Fuller, rushed "down under." Assembled at Seymour, Victoria, on April 14, 1942, they were reviewed by grateful Australia's minister for the Army Frank Forde.

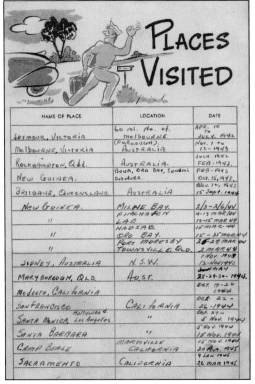

PLACES VISITED

| NAME OF PLACE | LOCATION | DATE |
|---|---|---|
| SEYMOUR, VICTORIA | 60 mi. No. of. Melbourne | APR. 10 To JULY. 1942 |
| MELBOURNE, VICTORIA | (PUckwood). AUSTRALIA | Nov. 1 to 12 - 1943 |
| ROCKHAMPTON, Qld. | AUSTRALIA. | JULY 1942, FEB-1943. |
| NEW GUINEA. | BUNA, ORO BAY, Senami Dobodura. | FEB-1943. OCT. 15, 1943. |
| BRISBANE, QUEENSLAND. | AUSTRALIA | Nov. 1, 1943 15 Sept. 1944 |
| NEW GUINEA. | MILNE BAY. | 2/3 - 2/6/44 |
| " | FINCHAFEN | 4-13 MAR 44 |
| | LAE | 13-15 MAR 44 |
| | NADZAB. | 15 MAR. 44 |
| " | ORO BAY. | 15 - 25 MAR 44 |
| | PORT MORESBY | 26-28 MAR 44 |
| " | TOWNSVILLE, QLD. | 2 MAR 44 1 Nov. 1943 |
| SIDNEY, AUSTRALIA | N. S. W. | 12 Nov 1943 1 MAY |
| MARYBOROUGH, QLD. | AUST. | 28-29-30- 1944. |
| MODESTO, CALIFORNIA | | OCT. 14-22 1944 |
| SAN FRANCISCO | CALIFORNIA | OCT. 22 - 26 -1944 |
| SANTA MONICA, Los Angeles Hollywood | " | OCT. 27 - 5 Nov. 1944 |
| SANTA BARBARA | " | 5 Nov. 1944 15 NOV. 1944 |
| CAMP BEALE | MARYSVILLE CALIFORNIA | 15 NOV. 1944 20 Aug. 1945 |
| SACRAMENTO | CALIFORNIA | 9 Jan 1945 26 MAR 1945 |

At Seymour, Sgt. Hugh Williams of the 116th Medical Regiment began a log of his ports of call. The Sunsetters moved to New Guinea, where relentless fighting earned the nickname "Jungleers" from Gen. Douglas MacArthur. (Courtesy Hugh Williams family.)

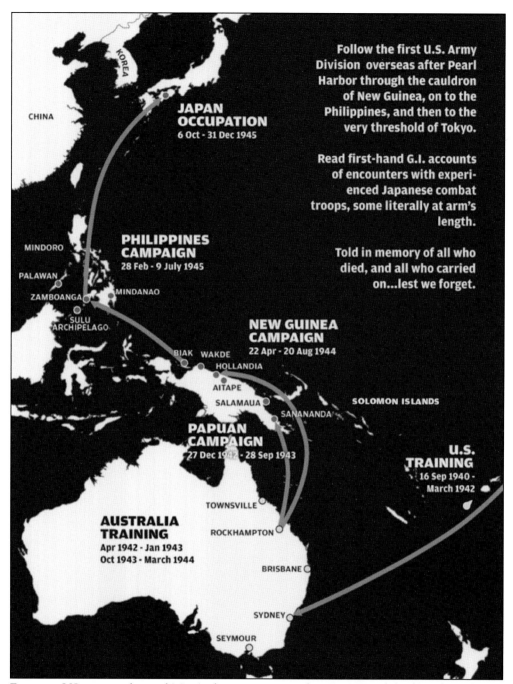

KOREA

CHINA

JAPAN
OCCUPATION
6 Oct - 31 Dec 1945

Follow the first U.S. Army
Division overseas after Pearl
Harbor through the cauldron
of New Guinea, on to the
Philippines, and then to the
very threshold of Tokyo.

Read first-hand G.I. accounts
of encounters with experienced Japanese combat
troops, some literally at arm's
length.

MINDORO

PALAWAN

ZAMBOANGA

SULU
ARCHIPELAGO

MINDANAO

PHILIPPINES
CAMPAIGN
28 Feb - 9 July 1945

Told in memory of all who
died, and all who carried
on...lest we forget.

NEW GUINEA
CAMPAIGN
22 Apr - 20 Aug 1944

BIAK  WAKDE
HOLLANDIA
AITAPE
SALAMAUA
SANANANDA

SOLOMON ISLANDS

PAPUAN
CAMPAIGN
27 Dec 1942 - 28 Sep 1943

U.S.
TRAINING
16 Sep 1940 -
March 1942

TOWNSVILLE

AUSTRALIA
TRAINING
Apr 1942 - Jan 1943
Oct 1943 - March 1944

ROCKHAMPTON

BRISBANE

SYDNEY

SEYMOUR

Emerging US strategy directed MacArthur to concurrently counterattack both in the Solomon
Islands and in northern New Guinea before jumping to the Philippines, eventually staging for
an invasion of the Japanese home islands. The 41st Division spearheaded the New Guinea and
Philippine campaigns, as shown. (Courtesy 41st Infantry Division Association.)

The Jungleers' toughest battle came on the island of Biak, where John Dawson of Battery A, 146th Field Artillery, stands at his gun (above) and rests at the "Biak Inn" (left). The division would next move to the island of Mindanao in the Southern Philippines. (Courtesy John Dawson family.)

Now commanded by Maj. Gen. Jens A. Doe, the Jungleers carried out Operation Victor IV, the seizure of Mindanao's Zamboanga peninsula, in March 1945 (above and below). Next would come the occupation of Japan. Counting that duty, the 41st Division clocked 45 months away from American soil, the longest overseas service of any American division. (Courtesy 41st Infantry Division Association.)

# CLASS "A" PASS

### FORTY - FIRST DIVISION, CAMP MURRAY, WASHINGTON

**Signature of Holder** — P.F.C. *Rene A. Peltier*

Name_ Rene A. Peltier, 20942890 _

Organization_ Co "B", 161st Inf (Rifle) _

Has permission to be absent from Camp Murray when not required for duty. Given in recognition of exemplary conduct.

Issued by_ *Capt J. R. Lee* _Comd'g_ Co B 161st _

Approved by Order of      1940-41

Colonel Orndorff _

*Ray L. Haynes* _      Feb 20/41 _

*Capt 161st Inf*     Adjutant     Date of Issue

The 161st Infantry Regiment and its parent 25th Infantry Division followed a somewhat different pathway. One wonders which experience Pfc. Rene Peltier enjoyed more: a pass to leave Camp Murray in the February 1941, or coast surveillance duty in Hawaii in February 1942. With Company B buddies "Bitch" Mendenall (left) and Conn Williams (right), Rene mans a gun position at Camp Bellows on Oahu's east coast. Later that month, all shifted a few miles south to Makapu'u Head, at the island's easternmost tip. But in November, war's reality would sink in when the 161st Infantry Regiment shipped out for Guadalcanal. (Courtesy Rene Peltier family.)

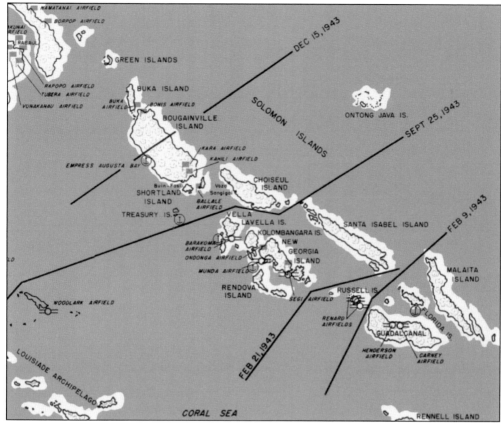

The 25th ("Tropic Lightning") Division's Solomon Island campaign worked in tandem with the Jungleers' slog across New Guinea (compare page 77). First Guadalcanal and then New Georgia to the northwest were their targets. American strategy dictated systematically retaking Japanese island strongholds, occupying airfields and naval installations, then vectoring toward the Philippines. (Courtesy 41st Infantry Division Association.)

When the 161st Regimental Combat Team (RCT) arrived at Guadalcanal in January 1943, the now-famous fight in the remote South Pacific had raged for five months. Their first mission was to eliminate Japanese troops at the Matanikau River Pocket. By February, with success imminent, their malaria-ridden commander, Col. Clarence Orndorff, had to be evacuated back home. Lt. Col. James Dalton took command. Dalton (left) directs planning for the RCT's landing on New Georgia on July 22. The brilliant Dalton would lead the 161st through relentless training and on to Luzon, where, tragically, he would be killed by a sniper at Balete Pass.

On New Georgia, 3rd Battalion, flanked by 1st Battalion, attacked Bartley's Ridge, then moved on to their next objective, Horseshoe Hill. As the battle progressed, weapons of every type, including machine guns, flamethrowers, and bazookas, came into play. The RCT cleared the hill, pillbox by pillbox, then closed on their final objective, Bibelot Hill.

Members of Company E gather in February 1943, shortly after their Guadalcanal victory. These same battle-hardened veterans would go on to win a Philippine Presidential Unit Citation for repelling a ferocious Japanese counterattack at San Manuel in Central Luzon.

With the battle for the Solomons won, the Tropic Lightning Division, including the 161st, sailed to New Zealand to recuperate and receive replacements and then spent the summer and fall of 1944 on the island of New Caledonia in intensive jungle training, which included practice in descending "scramble nets" into waiting landing craft.

In early 1945, the 161st returned to battle, joining a massive landing at Lingayen Gulf, Luzon. At first held in reserve, the RCT soon bulldozed into the interior. Hard fighting led to both Company E's heroic stand and Dalton's death. Another poignant note: the regiment fought not far from where its lineal ancestor had been sent a half-century before (Chapter 2). But this time, the mission was not to defeat the Filipino, but to fight with him to liberate his homeland. Indeed, just a year later, the Philippines finally became an independent republic.

On January 26, the 161st RCT finally crashed through San Manuel by sheer force of arms but then pivoted north to clear the Caraballo Mountains. Somewhere along the way, 13 soldiers, calling themselves the "Dirty Dozen," assembled. They were the last of the 161st Infantry's "old guard," who had fought together from the start (though two would not survive). Pictured from left to right are (first row) Thorkel Haaland (Pullman), Orville Camp (Bellingham), Glynn Wheeler (Kennewick), Alfred Finck (Spokane, killed in action [KIA]), George Russell (Bellingham), unidentified sergeant, Robert Speaks (Pullman), Robert MacCalder (Pullman, KIA), and Ross Haagland (Everett); (second row) Chuck Dougherty, Howard Murray (Bellingham), Willie Egbert (Seattle), and Bob Dickey (Walla Walla).

During its 39 months in the South Pacific, the 161st alone suffered more than 70 dead, plus General Dalton, with hundreds more wounded. Among the dead was a heroic medic, T/4 Laverne Parrish. When Company C's initial assault on San Manuel was temporarily repulsed, Parrish braved enemy fire to carry two wounded soldiers to safety. He went back to treat 12 others in full view of the enemy. Ultimately tending to nearly 40 soldiers, he was still moving among the battlefield wounded when an enemy mortar round landed in their midst. Parrish was mortally wounded. For his heroism, Laverne Parrish was posthumously awarded the Medal of Honor.

Other Washington Guard units served elsewhere. The 116th Observation Squadron, still operating the North American O-74, was reassigned in September 1941 from the 41st Division to the 2nd Air Force. They remained based at Gray Field at Fort Lewis but moved frequently, first to Yakima and Hoquiam, then to Corvallis, Oregon, and finally to Oklahoma City. Disbanded in November 1943, its personnel were reassigned to other units.

With its National Guard now in federalized status, the state needed a backup organized militia. A mere month after the September 1940 call-up, and immediately after enabling federal legislation, Washington created a home defense force, officially designated Washington State Guard. It comprised an infantry regiment, a home defense engineer battalion, a home defense antiaircraft battalion, and a home defense antitank battalion, plus a radio intelligence company and cavalry troop. By mid-1942, Washington State Guard strength stood at 150 officers and nearly 4,000 enlisted men. Somewhat belying this recruiting display, members were often older men not eligible for federal service.

Another war raged in Europe, of course; the Washington Guard was there, too. The 803rd Tank Destroyer Battalion sailed to Europe in June 1943 and fought in the Normandy, Northern France, Ardennes, Central Europe, and Rhineland campaigns. Company C (formerly 41st Division Tank Company) received the Presidential Unit Citation for action in the Hurtgen Forest, Germany. Other elements fought at the Battle of the Bulge, in Luxembourg and southern Germany, as well as in Austria and western Czechoslovakia. The emblem of the tank destroyers was a panther biting the tracks of a tank in half. (Courtesy Jody Harmon Military Prints and Gallery.)

Their basic weapon was the M10 Tank Destroyer, or "3-inch Gun Motor Carriage M10." It operated on the same drive train as the M4 Sherman Tank, which made it extremely dependable.

The 803rd claimed a sad distinction. Pfc. Charley Havlat, born to Czech immigrants in Nebraska, served with the Battalion through its bloodiest battles. On the morning of May 7, 1945, Havlat's reconnaissance platoon was blindsided by a hail of machine gun and small arms fire from concealed positions. Havlat took a bullet to the head, ending his life. That last firefight erupted less than 10 minutes after a general cease fire order and a mere six hours before Germany's unconditional surrender. (Neither German ambushers nor American tankers had heard the news.) Havlat died in his parents' native land, the last American killed in action in Europe during World War II.

Two future adjutants general served in World War II. Ensley M. Llewellyn began his Washington National Guard career in legendary Troop B, 58th Machine Gun Squadron, in Tacoma. He was appointed first sergeant in 1927, took a commission, and in 1943 attained lieutenant colonel. By that time working for Gen. Dwight Eisenhower, he was directed to initiate the famous World War II newspaper *Stars and Stripes*. The first edition, published in London, was a highly successful eight-page weekly, prompting Eisenhower to request it become a daily. Its substantial profits were turned over to the Army welfare fund. At the D-Day landing, Llewellyn was in the twelfth wave. In the town of Carentan, he commandeered the local printshop, over which he raised a Carentan sign maker's banner reading "Stars and Stripes Continental Edition." In 1947, he was appointed brigadier general and Washington's adjutant general.

Lilburn H. Stevens, born September 2, 1902, in Liberal, Kansas, joined the Army in 1918, serving with the 28th Infantry Division in most of the western-front campaigns. A few years after the war, he enlisted in the Washington National Guard as a private in the 41st Tank Company in Centralia. By World War II, he was executive officer of the 803rd Tank Destroyer Battalion. After his second war, he returned to the Washington Guard, becoming adjutant general in August 1949, eventually retiring in 1957 as a major general.

# Seven

# COLD WAR,
# VICTORY TO VIETNAM
## 1946 TO 1961

Victory brought the boys home again, and again, it took time to reconstitute. Back to its Northwest states came the 41st Division, now reunited with its old 161st Infantry. A growth spurt followed. The Army National Guard gained new members, new units, and new technology requiring new armories. And a new Washington Air National Guard was born when a separate US Air Force was created in 1947.

A new global peril accelerated the reconfiguration: the onset of a fearsome Cold War between erstwhile allies, the United States and Soviet Russia. A new arms race erupted. Shockingly, Russia tested an atomic device in 1949.

America suddenly needed a comprehensive air defense program. Recalling the coast artillery era, national security strategists turned to the Guard. Since the jet age made antiaircraft artillery inadequate, the United States, starting in 1954, lined its coasts with surface-to-air missiles to intercept any air attack. For the next two decades, Guardsmen manned the sites ringing Puget Sound around the clock. And the Air Guard added an interceptor capability.

Meanwhile, a new land war in Asia punctuated the Cold War face-off. North Korea invaded the South in 1950. Pres. Harry Truman activated several Washington Guard units: 66th Field Artillery Group, 420th Antiaircraft Artillery Battalion, and, most importantly, the Washington Air Guard. The latter's 116th Fighter Interceptor Squadron became America's first jet fighter/interceptor unit to cross an ocean. But it flew the Atlantic to England with a mission to beef up America's forces there to deter any Russian mischief. A negotiated cease-fire brought the units back in February 1953.

Nature did not pause for geopolitics. An unusually heavy snowpack led to devastating spring floods in the Columbia Basin in 1948. About 500 Washington Guardsmen activated to shore up dikes and levees. But the waters remained high for weeks, and the toll was grim.

Through the era, the Army and Air National Guard trained for a third world war that, fortunately, never came. To provide homegrown leadership, Washington State, under federal guidance, established a Washington Military Academy in 1957. It commissioned its first second lieutenants the next May, the first class of Washington Guard officers in a program that still flourishes.

In 1961, John Kennedy took over the presidency from Dwight Eisenhower, the former general who led the Cold War strategies of the 1950s. A series of crises confronted the young leader in Cuba, in Berlin, and above all, in Southeast Asia. The Guard would play a different role.

With return and reconstitution, training resumed. In 1950, troops from the 41st Division converged by rail for training at Camp Murray.

As peacetime training routines settled in, recruiting resumed. The Sears, Roebuck & Company store in downtown Tacoma featured a prominent and patriotic display. The soldier, stacked rifles, and flag dramatized the appeal to enroll at the local Tacoma armory. A prospective private would "learn and earn" a whopping $2 each weekly three-hour drill! (Courtesy Tacoma Public Library.)

The Guard—it's a gig! Some postwar enlistees went on to become music legends—first in the Seattle club scene and then nationwide. A little-known but extraordinary story is that, in 1947–1948, the 41st Division Band was an all–African American group led by Guard warrant officer Robert "Bumps" Blackwell (far left). Seattle-born Blackwell (1918–1985) was an American bandleader, songwriter, arranger, and record producer. He groomed and publicized such headline artists as Little Richard, Ray Charles, Ernestine Anderson, Lloyd Price, Sam Cooke, Herb Alpert, Larry Williams, Sly and the Family Stone, and Quincy Jones. Jones played in Blackwell's 41st band; he stands in the left-most column, second from back.

Winter 1947–1948 brought unusually heavy snows; sudden late spring warmth and rains thawed the snowpack, rapidly bloating the Columbia River. From the Hanford Works in the Tri-Cities area to the shipbuilding complexes and lumber mills of the lower river, the war had industrialized the Columbia. Previous floods were worse in water volume, but this one inflicted a crushing toll of 50 deaths, 46,000 homes destroyed, and over $100 million in damage. Most spectacularly, it destroyed the new town of Vanport, Oregon. Five hundred Washington Guardsmen tried to save the dike at Woodland. They failed and, in the process, saw two of their bulldozers sink in the muck. (Courtesy Clark County Historical Museum, cchm04083.tif and CMOS00518.tif.)

Other Guard heavy equipment did make a difference, aiding evacuation of residents and then guarding their property. A star of the service was an icon of the late war: the amphibious vehicle, or DUKW. Affectionately known as a "Duck," of course, it was a six-wheel drive 2.5-ton military truck modified for water-to-land flexibility. Used extensively in World War II and again in Korea, DUKWs survived in limited military use for a while, and more recently as a tourist attraction. As for the misbehaving river, its flooding is now under control thanks to a United States–Canada treaty in 1961. A response to the 1948 disaster, it directed construction of three storage dams north of the border.

The old 116th Observation Squadron was reactivated at Felts Field in 1946 with a new mission of flying fighters. Its first aircraft was the World War II workhorse, the P-51 Mustang. But in 1949, it became the first Guard squadron west of the Mississippi River to be equipped with jets. And with the creation of a separate US Air Force, the squadron became the flagship of the new Washington *Air* National Guard. The postwar Air Guard gained new missions and new aircraft, appropriate to its new alignment with the nation's Strategic Air Command. The Air Guard still flew the old reliable C-47 (Douglas DC-3, above), a proven transport since 1941, but soon gained the Republic E-84 Thunder Jet. Then came the new North American F-86 Sabre, shown below in 1955 with pilot and maintainers doing their preflight checks. By then, the 116th had moved to Geiger Field (present-day Spokane International Airport), with its needed longer runways.

The Lockheed T-33 Shooting Star ("T-Bird") was a subsonic American jet trainer, which first flew in 1948. The 116th Fighter Squadron trained on the T-Bird from 1948 until the mid-1970s.

With the outbreak of the Korean Conflict, the 116th Fighter Interceptor Squadron went back to war. In fact, it accomplished America's first jet fighter/interceptor transoceanic flight. But not to Korea. Instead, it flew the Atlantic to England to bolster NATO's European deterrent. Lt. Col. Frank Frost, 116th commander, led the historic flight. Why the 116th? Frost's answer was to "show the Russians what the US reserve force could do."

This was the sleek airplane that the 116th took to England. The North American F-86 Sabre, a transonic jet fighter aircraft, was the nation's first swept-wing fighter. So successful was the

"Sabrejet" that more than 7,800 aircraft were delivered between 1949 and 1956. The 116th flew it through 1955.

The 116th's historic transatlantic flight was also the first time that a National Guard fighter squadron crossed to the European theater under its own power, and without air refueling. The unit was based at rural Shepherds Grove in Suffolk, England, staged to support the new NATO alliance forces. Quonset huts served as the squadron's headquarters, operations center, and living quarters. From left to right at Hut No. 499 are (first row) Bill Benway, Dick Thiele, and Dick Ward; (second row) George Mitchell, Dale Wainwright, and Bill Bronkhorst; (third row) Chas Miller, Ed Palum, Earl Salmonson, Dick Eacho, Dick Cranston, and Ed Warford; (fourth row) Jack Bradley, Alton Cook, Bob Graft, Bill Davis, Richard Flynn, and Don Odell. Wainwright went on to become wing commander and a brigadier general before retiring in 1985.

In November 1952, the squadron's active-duty tour ended. Three years after returning to Geiger Field, they received a new plane: the Lockheed F-94B Starfire. This aircraft expanded the squadron's mission from day interceptor to day-and-night all-weather interceptor.

The Army, too, took to the skies in the 1950s. Army aviation is best known for rotary-wing aircraft: helicopters in many sizes and uses. The H-21 Workhorse/Shawnee was nicknamed the "Flying Banana"; Piasecki Helicopter (later Boeing Vertol) built this tandem rotor helicopter. Another Guard "bird" was the OH-23 Raven, a three-seat, light observation helicopter first flown in 1948.

To defend against enemy airpower, the Army National Guard manned antiaircraft missile installations. The Nike Ajax was the world's first operational surface-to-air missile (SAM), entering service in 1954. The missile targeted conventional bombers flying at high subsonic speeds at altitudes above 50,000 feet. The Washington Guard operated 10 Ajax sites by 1958. In 1963, the Nike Hercules (SAM-A-25, later M/M-14) replaced the Ajax; the Washington Guard operated two Nike Hercules sites at Redmond and Vashon Island until 1974. The long-range air defense mission of the command-guided "Herc" included a nuclear warhead that could destroy entire formations of high-altitude supersonic attackers.

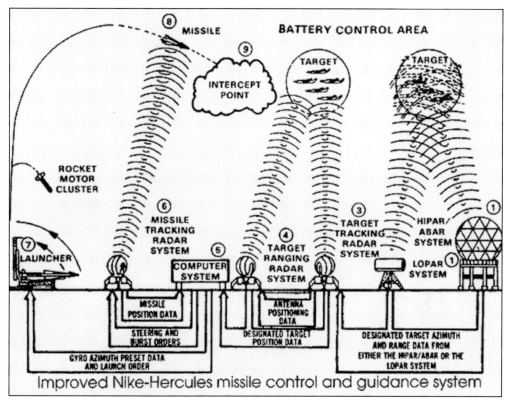

Improved Nike-Hercules missile control and guidance system

A complete system included radars and computers as well as the missile and launchers. At the Midway site in 1958, a missile technician brings an Ajax from an underground magazine to a rail system above for loading onto a launcher.

Army ground troops likewise worked with various kinds of equipment, some current, some hand-me-downs from the active Army, all periodically upgraded. The World War II–era M-4 Sherman tank remained a Washington Guard battle weapon into the 1950s. Crews trained at Fort Lewis and the firing center north of Yakima. The 75-millimeter or 105-millimeter main gun, backed up by a 50-caliber or 30-caliber machine gun, required a crew of five.

Regularly scheduled full-scale training in the field prepared a new generation of soldiers in skills their older comrades had learned in combat. In 1953, the 803rd Tank Battalion finds out if their crews can coordinate the many aspects of their tactical craft.

Many different specialties mesh to form a well-supported combat operation. But every soldier, from cook to clerk to communicator, is first an infantryman. So, marksmanship has always been a hallmark of military training. The M1 Garand, the US service rifle during World War II and Korea, remained the primary individual weapon through the 1950s.

The integrated modern battlefield required skilled operators of sophisticated "commo" gear. One system for communicating in the field was the radio and radioteletype shelter, commonly referred to as a "*RATT RIG.*" These cramped trucks or vans housed radioteletype (RTTY) systems: two or more electromechanical teleprinters linked by radio rather than wire.

In 1957, the Washington Guard established the Washington Military Academy to prepare its own for officer commissions. The National Guard Bureau wanted to replace extension courses with an aggressive resident training program in each state. Fifteen days of annual active training and 10 two-day weekend assemblies added up to 350 hours of training, divided between academic subjects and leadership training. Thirty-five young Guardsmen received their lieutenant's bars from the first class in 1958. At the same time, enlisted soldiers received more formalized, mandatory active-duty training: eight weeks of basic combat training plus six weeks unit training. Cold War threats required skilled soldiers and well-prepared leaders. So did the whirlwind events of the turbulent 1960s and beyond.

# Eight

# Cold War,
# Vietnam to Victory
## 1962 to 1989

As the 1960s unfolded, the American commitment to fighting in Vietnam dwarfed other defense priorities. What distinguished this from previous wars was that it was fought primarily by draftees, not mobilized Guard soldiers. Thus, many draft-eligible men escaped a call by joining the Guard, eroding its morale and discipline.

As it endured its role as a refuge, the Washington Guard slowly changed. The historic 41st Infantry Division was broken up into its respective state components. In Washington, the 81st Infantry Brigade emerged as the umbrella command. The Guard's air defense mission phased out. The Air Guard converted from fighter interceptors to air refueling tankers.

Conversely, a new organization brought back an older mission—the Army National Guard found itself back at sea with a watercraft transportation battalion, owning several different vessels.

Then, in the 1970s, out of the ashes of America's final withdrawal from Vietnam, arose a new role for the Guard. It was part of a new national strategy that led, stunningly within 15 years, to the end of the Cold War, indeed the collapse of the arch-adversary, the Soviet Union. The Army chief of staff, Gen. Creighton Abrams, determined that the Guard should never again be sidelined. Not to call on citizen soldiers was to forfeit the engagement of America's citizens.

Henceforth, a new all-volunteer Total Force doctrine would knit the Guard into active Army plans and structures. Added funding and new equipment came to the state; new functions like combat engineering and chemical detection fell to Guard formations; a direct affiliation with Fort Lewis's active 9th Infantry Division began. This relentless rebuilding and integration of American military strength accelerated through the 1980s. Indirectly at least, it contributed to the Cold War "victory" the United States celebrated when in 1989 the Berlin Wall fell and the Soviet Union dissolved.

A more integral operational role and higher readiness standards did not exempt the Washington Guard from its domestic duties. Guardsmen, and now Guardswomen, responded to a drumbeat of call-ups for familiar disturbances and disasters. But few armies in history have ever had to confront what Washington soldiers and airmen fought in 1980: the aftermath of the explosive eruption of Mount St. Helens—the deadliest and most economically destructive volcanic event in US history. Search and rescue, ash cleanup, and patrols of roads and facilities required a massive turnout—almost all volunteer.

This part of the Guard's historic dual mission never changes. The 21st century would prove that dictum.

For Washington State, the era began on a celebratory note with the opening of the Seattle World's Fair in 1962. The Guard contributed its armory, shown in 1961 behind the legs of the rising Space Needle; it was reconfigured for the fair into an innovative vertical shopping mall, called the Food Circus. Built in 1939 to house field artillery, the armory has always served as a versatile community gathering place, and to this day it attracts thousands of visitors at the heart of the Seattle Center. (Courtesy MOHAI, Seattle Post-Intelligencer Collection, 1986.5.27974.4.)

A Vietnam-era icon, the UH-1 "Huey" symbolizes both what the Washington Guard did not do and what it did. By the early 1970s, a second Army aviation flight facility was added in Spokane, bolstering the Gray Field operation at Fort Lewis. Army National Guard pilots flew both the Huey and the OH-58 Kiowa, not in Vietnam but in support of government agencies and civilian organizations.

The war came home in episodes of unrest in the streets. Guard soldiers were drawn into conflict with their contemporaries. Civil disturbance training became a requirement.

It was the end of an era as the 41st Infantry Division fully inactivated by 1968. Its last commanding general was Maj. Gen. Ralph Phelps, who began as a private in 1936 with Company B, 161st Infantry Regiment. He rose through the ranks and was commissioned second lieutenant in 1940. With the 161st in World War II, he proved an effective combat leader from company commander to battalion executive officer, earning the Bronze Star as well as many other awards. He reentered the Guard as commander, 1st Battalion, 161st Infantry, eventually rising to battle group commander, assistant division commander, and finally, division commander in June 1962.

A "navy" returned to the Army National Guard in 1963 in the form of a terminal operations battalion. It boasted landing craft, harbor and ocean tugs, a freight ship, a 250-foot floating machine shop, and an assortment of barges and cranes, plus small passenger craft known as "picket" boats. The 176-foot FS-313 seagoing freight ship *Betsy Ross* sailed for 25 years with the battalion. One of her many tasks was to load landing craft for a tactic called "LOTS," a military acronym for Logistics-Over-The-Shore, i.e. where no port facilities exist. Struck from the Army registry in the late 1990s, the *Betsy Ross* is flagged in Panama today and continues to work.

Unlike the old Naval Militia, the 144th Transportation Battalion (Terminal) had a real wartime mission: to manage pre-positioned materiel in ports around the world. Operating from the Tacoma waterfront, its vessels cruised from Puget Sound all the way to Alaska. The 74-foot LCM-8, or "Mike Boat," was a mechanized landing craft used by both Army and Navy. It weighed 135,000 pounds and had a crew of four. Above, infantry soldiers are put ashore in training exercises at Solo Point on Puget Sound near Steilacoom in the late 1960s.

The 100-foot LT 2076 ("Large Tug-Seagoing"), named the *New Guinea*, was the workhorse of the 144th fleet until, in 1995, the entire battalion was reassigned to the US Army Reserve.

It was the end of an era for the Air Guard in 1976 when, after three decades, the 116th left the fighter business to take on the mission of aerial refueling. Their F-101 Voodoos (right) were exchanged for KC135A Refuelers (left). Thereafter, both Air Guard and US Air Force aircraft would happily greet the extended fuel boom from the "flying gas station" (see page 120), offered by what was now designated the 141st Air Refueling Wing.

Another "end of an era" came in 1974 when Nike air defense missile sites in Washington deactivated. Each unit's equipment, from radars to massive generators, were crated and trucked to Army depots, and the land was given to community organizations. For instance, remaining buildings at the Vashon Island site now house a thrift store, Vashon Health clinic, and a radio station; launchpads, covered with soil, have become the Paradise Ridge Park equestrian area.

What never changed through the decades was proficiency training on a variety of weapons systems. The 105-millimeter M40 recoilless rifle (above) was a jeep-mounted antitank weapon. It found domestic use in the Cascade mountains for avalanche mitigation. An engineering unit (below) could also find a civilian application, like assisting in a road project to sharpen soldier skills.

**One weekend with the Guard buys you anything here.**

How would you like to earn about $40 real quick? For clothes, good times, or anything you want.

Well you can make over $40 by spending just one weekend a month with the National Guard.

You'll get a chance to learn a trade or skill, to do something different once a month—and still enjoy your regular civilian life.

And you'll be doing something important. Because the Guard belongs to the country as part of our national defense force. And to the community as an aid in emergencies.

Send for details about the Army National Guard or Air National Guard and the many ways the Guard can pay off for you.

National Guard Bureau, Room IE-467
The Pentagon, Washington, D.C. 20310

Gentlemen: Please send me information about ☐ Army National Guard
☐ Air National Guard          J426

Name                                Age

Address

City              State              Zip

**national guard**

The Guard belongs.

Cringeworthy stereotypes appear in this 1975 nationally produced recruiting display advertisement. Were prospective recruits really enticed by these trinkets at the end of the divisive Vietnam War?

More likely, it was the training that appealed the most to young men and women. The Washington Guard offered technical and mechanical skill development that translated to jobs in the working world. Truck, helicopter, and even heavy tank maintenance could aid the employment search. Office, medical, or other professional assignments could be more prized than the paycheck.

Women were also responding to new opportunities offered by the Guard. The Washington Guard was among the earliest to welcome female members. Gov. Dan Evans swore in the Washington Guard's first female soldier, SP5 Nora Campbell, in October 1972. Others rapidly followed.

In the closing days of the war, thousands of Vietnamese fled their homeland. Washington governor Dan Evans chose to provide temporary housing for some of the refugees at Camp Murray. The Guard headquarters had facilities, feeding capability, and seclusion. The Vietnamese Assistance Center also provided offices for interviews and placement. The Red Cross and the Salvation Army, as well as community volunteers, came together to help; by the time the center closed on Camp Murray in 1975, about 640 future American citizens had passed through.

Visitors from VIETNAM

After months of rumbling, Mount St. Helens in southwest Washington let loose. The Guard had already been activated to help civil authorities cordon off areas around the mountain. But no one anticipated the sideways blast that blew up 2,000 feet of mountaintop on a pleasant Sunday morning in May 1980. Fortunately, the Guard's helicopters, in Yakima for annual training, launched when, as pilot Hal Kolb remembered, "We walked outside and could see this 80,000-foot wall of ash churning like an avalanche." The choppers flew into a moonscape to rescue survivors. This Washington Huey settles in deep ash above what is left of Spirit Lake.

That fateful morning, Sue Ruff and Bruce Nelson were lost, disoriented, and frightened when they heard Mike Cairns's helicopter. Mike landed and followed footprints in the ash until he found the pair. Soon, Sue (as well as Bruce and their dog) buckled in for the flight to safety. 37 years later, after Sue had completed her own National Guard career in Oregon, she and Mike would be reunited thanks to the PBS documentary series *We'll Meet Again*, hosted by Ann Curry.

Over several weeks, 16 aircraft flew 400 missions; in the first three days, 163 people were rescued. Guard pilot Harold Kolb talked with an unidentified truck driver before lifting him out of the debris and flying him to safety at the Kelso Airport. He was lucky; 57 perished in the eruption.

Gov. Dixie Lee Ray ordered immediate cleanup in the swath of Eastern Washington buried under up to seven inches of dense ash. Guard members from across the state brought equipment from hand shovels and wheelbarrows to backhoes and dump trucks. One of many detachments "hauling ash" (in classic soldier lingo), the 141st Air Refueling Wing clears the heavy stuff from a rooftop in peril.

In the 1980s, the Washington Guard increasingly took part in humanitarian training missions overseas. In the Panamanian jungle, watercraft operators delivered heavy engineer equipment for a road building initiative, nicknamed "Blazing Trails," on the remote Azuero Peninsula.

As the Total Force concept became reality by the 1980s, Washington Guard units trained with US and Allied armies around the world, including NATO's REFORGER exercise (REturn of FORces to GERmany) and the United States–Japan Defense Force Command Post Exercise YAMA SAKURA. The various exercises and deployments were precursors to the post–Cold War world that lay ahead. Beginning in 1990 the Washington Guard found itself with "boots on the ground" in combat zones and disaster areas. As a new century approached, the future held both great promise and great peril.

## Nine

# COLD WAR TO WAR ON TERROR
## 1990 TO PRESENT

As the Cold War came to an end, the Washington Guard continued to be organized as a strategic reserve. In early 1990, when Iraq invaded Kuwait, the Guard began to sense how important "strategic reserve" had become in the nation's defense. Army and Air Guard units were immediately called, the first activations since the Korean conflict.

The Guard moved quickly to become an "operational reserve." In 1997, Washington's Air Guard assumed the Western Air Defense Sector mission, safeguarding America's western skies. Units and individuals served rotations as multinational peacekeepers and observers in the Balkans and the Middle East.

Throughout the 1990s, the Washington Guard continued to assist in flood recovery and wildland firefighting, and joined law enforcement in quelling civil unrest. As the decade ended, the Guard was mobilized to help control rioting and demonstrations against the World Trade Organization (WTO) Conference in Seattle, dubbed the "Battle of Seattle."

The new century seemed to dawn quietly. Then came September 11, 2001, and the Guard's world changed again. A new priority, "Homeland Security," provided missions the Guard had never imagined. Since 2001, the Washington Guard has deployed over 15,000 soldiers and airmen to 25 countries globally as part of US military operations in Afghanistan, East Africa, the Middle East, the Philippines, and elsewhere.

Nor did natural disasters let up. The Washington Guard was there for Louisianans when Hurricanes Rita and Katrina hit in 2005 and for their own neighbors in 2014 when a mudslide buried the Washington town of Oso.

Nearly three decades since the fall of the Berlin Wall, the Washington Guard has continued its commitment to hometowns, communities, state, nation, and its international partners across the globe. But at its root, it is still a community-based force, dedicated to a safe and secure Washington State. Recruited locally in communities and for communities, Guard members engage every aspect of life in their hometowns. From aiding food drives and drug reduction programs to mitigating disasters and rescuing victims, they truly are "citizens serving citizens."

And no end is in sight. Whether down the street or across the globe, in armed combat teams or in humanitarian relief efforts, these "part-time soldiers" still ready themselves for anything—24 hours a day, seven days a week.

Washington Air National Guard members board a KC-135 aircraft bound for the Middle East Tuesday at Fairchild Air Force Base. *Staff photo by Colin Mulvany*

## Guard group takes off for Middle East

The first mobilizations for overseas combat duty since the Korean War occurred in 1990 when the United States built a coalition force after Iraq invaded Kuwait. Army National Guard transportation, personnel, and support operations units, as well as most of the 141st Air Refueling Wing, plus dozens of individual volunteers, mobilized and deployed to Operations Desert Shield and Desert Storm. Here, Air Guard members load up to head to the Middle East. (Courtesy Archives/ *The Spokesman Review.*)

Later in the 1990s, the Guard was called upon to assist with peacekeeping duties in the Balkans. Following the dissolution of Yugoslavia, the Republic of Bosnia proclaimed independence in 1992, followed by the Bosnian War lasting until late 1995. In December 1995, under Operation Joint Endeavor, NATO deployed multinational peacekeeping forces; in December 1996, remaining troops transferred to a Stabilization Force (SFOR). SFOR peacekeepers stayed in Bosnia until 2004. In 1997, members of the 122nd Public Affairs Detachment joined allied peacekeepers on patrol in Bosnia.

As had been the practice in the Guard for many years, preparing for and assisting in wildland firefighting continued throughout the decade. With disciplined crews and self-sustaining capabilities, the Guard was the "support of choice" across the state. Here, soldiers from Tacoma deploy water delivered from an all-terrain M939 five-ton six-by-six US military heavy truck.

In November 1999, the World Trade Organization (WTO) held its conference in Seattle. Protests followed meetings of such international organizations, and this meeting was no different. More than 40,000 activists converged outside the conference venues. After the protests turned violent, the Guard, responding to a call from the governor, took to the streets in full riot gear alongside law enforcement. These protests were the subject of the 2007 film *Battle in Seattle*. (Courtesy Christopher J. Morris - Corbis, via Getty Images.)

In the early morning hours of September 11, 2001, the Western Air Defense Sector (WADS)was engaged in a North American Aerospace Defense Command (NORAD) exercise watching the skies over the Western United States. The day suddenly became anything but routine. Shortly after the attacks on the World Trade Center and the Pentagon occurred, NORAD ordered the airspace closed. WADS swung into action and cleared the skies. They then launched and controlled the combat air patrols over major Western cities. In this photograph, representative of the emergency actions performed that day, S.Sgt. Lara Koler, an identification technician, tracks radar targets to identify "tracks of interest." (Courtesy US Air Force photograph/Randy Rubattino.)

The entire US military jumped into action after 9/11. With the immediate need for fighter aircraft to fly continuous missions over US cities, Washington's KC-135 air refueling fleet responded. Here, an F16 is pulling up for gas. Fighters and their "refuelers" flew thousands of hours of critical mission time in what was called "CAP," or combat air patrol. CAP entails fighters flying a tactical pattern around or screening a defended target, while looking for potential incoming threats.

Following the attacks, the president ordered the National Guard to assist with securing the nation's airports until the new Transportation Security Administration (TSA) could take over the duties. The presence of the Guard provided a comforting presence for air travelers, while also maintaining security oversight at the airport's security checkpoints. These Guardsmen from Yakima enjoyed interacting with local airport passengers while taking this job very seriously.

In February 2002, the Winter Olympics got under way in Salt Lake City, and officials promised the heaviest security ever for a sporting event. That included up to 15,000 soldiers, federal agents, state and local police, and private security staff. Washington's contribution included these soldiers from Troop E, 303rd Cavalry—modern-day descendants of the legendary Troop B from Tacoma.

"Today we honor you—You are our heroes," Gov. Gary Locke told the troops. At the February 2004 departure ceremony for Washington's 81st Armor Brigade, it was quite a scene. Their deployment, the biggest for the Washington Guard since World War II, was about to begin. The crowd nearly filled the 15,000 seats set up for them. The 4,200 members of the brigade stood in formation on the floor of the Tacoma Dome, during the two-hour event. As the names of the 33 states' units were read out, the soldiers barked "Hoo-ah!" while the crowd cheered. "We are one Army—active, guard, and reserve. We're in this together," said Gen. Edward Soriano, commander of Fort Lewis. The deployment lasted 18 months, with 12 months in Iraq and the US Central Command area of operations.

Washington's largest single unit, the 81st Brigade, one of the US Army's 15 National Guard "enhanced readiness," or E-brigades, had been activated in November 2003 to support Operation Iraqi Freedom. Most of its troops conducted pre-mobilization training at Fort Lewis, Washington, and the National Training Center in California. The brigade deployed again in 2008. During that deployment, the focus of the brigade was security and "force protection operations." The 81st today is known as a "Stryker Brigade Combat Team," or SBCT, utilizing the Stryker "armored fighting vehicle," and is affiliated with the 2nd Infantry Division.

Despite ongoing deployments supporting the Global War on Terror, the Air Guard's 254th Red Horse Squadron (Rapid Engineer Deployable Heavy Operational Repair Squadron Engineer), some recently returned from a deployment to the Horn of Africa supporting Operation Enduring Freedom, lent their construction and engineering expertise to the preparations for the 200th anniversary of the Lewis and Clark Expedition, a precursor to Washington State's creation.

Members of the Washington Army and Air National Guard deployed in the aftermath of Hurricane Katrina. While members from both, including some recently returned from Iraq, formed a task force to provide direct, on-the-ground support, the 141st Air Refueling Wing provided transport for the task force and for moving supplies from all over the Pacific Northwest. The 66th Theater Aviation Command deployed helicopters to help with search, rescue, recovery, and supply delivery. Here, the soldier is helping residents recover important belongings.

While deployed in support of the Global War on Terror, some units were called on to perform an overseas mission for which the Guard is better qualified than the active forces—support to civil authorities following disasters. Above, in 2005, the CH-47 Chinook helicopters of Company B, 168th Aviation, move relief supplies following a 7.6 magnitude earthquake that struck the Kashmir region of Pakistan, while they were deployed to Afghanistan to fight the Taliban.

In 2004, a member of the Washington Army National Guard provides first aid to an injured person following devastating floods that struck the country of Djibouti. He was deployed with his unit to East Africa to fight transnational terrorism.

As it has for the last 160 years, the Guard continues to be called upon to help support and protect their state, while continuing as an operational reserve of the nation's military. The single deadliest landslide in US history took place on March 22, 2014, near the small town of Oso, Washington. In total, 43 people were killed and 49 homes destroyed. By March 25, the Guard deployed a search-and-extraction team and a fatality search-and-recovery team from the Air National Guard 141st Civil Engineer Squadron. Later, decontamination teams from the Army National Guard 790th Chemical Company, stationed in nearby Snohomish, were sent in. This was truly a case of neighbors helping neighbors!

Here, Guard members take a well-deserved break from wildland firefighting in 2014. Guard troops have performed tens of thousands of man-hours conducting wildland firefighting and support missions across the region. Hundreds of Guard members have trained for and assisted in firefighting over recent decades, as well as supporting flood recovery, snow removal, evacuation, and other disaster response and mitigation activities.

The Guard not only serves state and nation during times of strife, unrest, and war, but also when the community calls for something completely different. When the Seattle Seahawks won Superbowl XLVIII in February 2014, the team and the city asked the Washington National Guard to provide transportation for the celebratory parade.

Guard missions are highly diversified in today's modern military. Dozens of states' National Guards conduct unique partnerships with foreign nation's military for the purpose of security cooperation and mutually beneficial training. Washington is a partner with both the Kingdom of Thailand and the country of Malaysia. During a visit, senior Thai officers are briefed by the Washington Army Guard deputy chief of staff for joint operations, Col. Kevin McMahan, and the Washington Air Guard commander, Brig. Gen. Jeremy Horn.

# About the Washington National Guard State Historical Society

The preceding images provide a brief view of the rich history of the Washington National Guard. The photograph below shows the exterior of "the Arsenal," which houses much, much more of the history and is the home of the Washington National Guard State Historical Society Museum. Visit us in person, or online at www.waguardmuseum.org, or on Facebook at www.facebook/wngshs.

The Washington National Guard State Historical Society (WNGSHS) was founded in 1989 by a group of dedicated current and former members of the Washington National Guard who had a joint interest in collecting, preserving, and exhibiting the heritage of Washington's militia and National Guard. They hope to further educate, through informative displays and exhibits, the rich and fascinating stories of the local military men and women of the Pacific Northwest.

The WNG Museum is an activity of the Washington National Guard and the Washington Military Department and is operated under agreement by the Washington National Guard State Historical Society (WNGSHS), a nonprofit 501(c)(3) organization, registered with the State of Washington as a nonprofit corporation. The adjutant general serves as registered agent of the corporation.

The museum is recognized by the National Guard Bureau and the US Army Center for Military History and is supported in part by annual contributions from private, corporate, and foundation funds. The museum is a member of the American Association for State and Local History, Washington Museum Association, and the Pierce County Heritage Alliance.

Building 2, Militia Drive
Camp Murray, WA 98430

Email: wngshs@live.com
Phone: (253) 512-7834

# DISCOVER THOUSANDS OF LOCAL HISTORY BOOKS FEATURING MILLIONS OF VINTAGE IMAGES

Arcadia Publishing, the leading local history publisher in the United States, is committed to making history accessible and meaningful through publishing books that celebrate and preserve the heritage of America's people and places.

Find more books like this at
**www.arcadiapublishing.com**

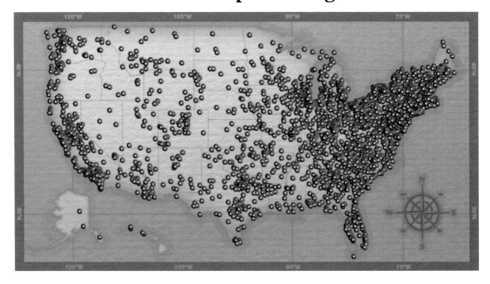

Search for your hometown history, your old stomping grounds, and even your favorite sports team.

Consistent with our mission to preserve history on a local level, this book was printed in South Carolina on American-made paper and manufactured entirely in the United States. Products carrying the accredited Forest Stewardship Council (FSC) label are printed on 100 percent FSC-certified paper.

MADE IN THE USA